EYEWITNESS

Question &Answer B·Q·O·&·O·A·K

Written by
John Farndon

DORLING KINDERSLEY
London • New York • Stuttgart

A DORLING KINDERSLEY BOOK

Managing editor Helen Parker
Managing art editor Julia Harris
Senior art editor Jill Plank
Designer Sharon Spencer
Design assistance Manisha Patel
Production Samantha Larmour

Why do butterflies have
markings on their wings?

What did the
ancient Greeks
keep in an
amphora?

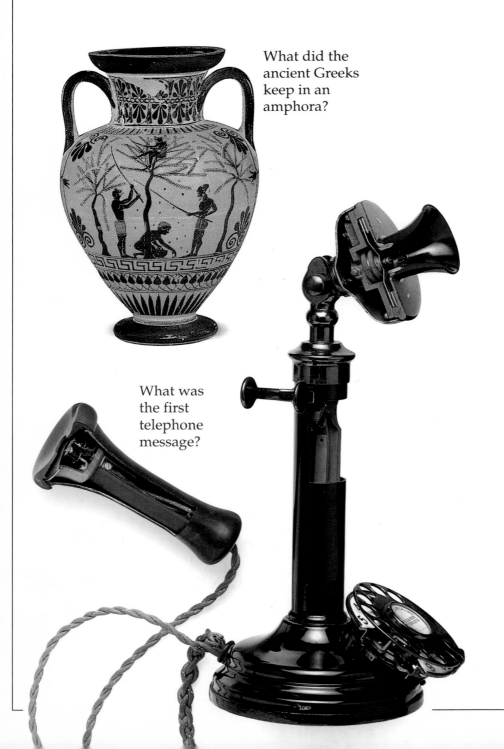

What was
the first
telephone
message?

This Eyewitness ® Guide has been
conceived by Dorling Kindersley Limited

First published in Great Britain in 1993
by Dorling Kindersley Limited
9 Henrietta Street, London WC2E 8PS

Copyright © 1993
Dorling Kindersley Limited
London

A CIP catalogue record for this book is
available from the British Library.

ISBN 0 7513 6016 3

Colour reproduction by
Colourscan, Singapore

Printed in Singapore
by Toppan

Contents

What do you know about nature?

6 Why is the Earth unique?

8 How are rocks formed?

10 Why are plants green?

12 How high are the world's tallest trees?

14 Why are some animals poisonous?

16 Why are polar bears white?

18 What do bones do?

20 What makes a home?

22 Who lays eggs?

What makes a home?

When did it happen?

26 When did life begin?

28 Where is the oldest town?

30 Who believed in gods?

32 Where is the Fertile Crescent?

34 Who were the first merchants?

36 How was the world explored?

38 Why wear clothes?

40 Who started athletics?

42 Who played a mammoth-bone flute?

Which beetle was sacred to the ancient Egyptians?

Why did the ancient Egyptians value the wedjat eye?

Who invented it?

46 Who made the first tools?

48 What was the first weapon?

50 Who was the first true doctor?

52 How fast can a message be sent?

54 Who invented movies?

56 What is natural energy?

58 How old is steam power?

60 Did cars or trains come first?

62 How do we fly?

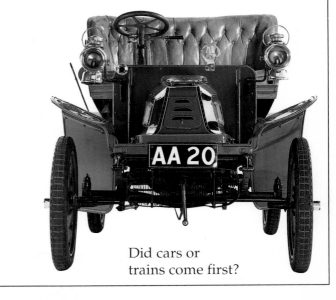

Did cars or trains come first?

64 Index

What do you know about nature?

THE NATURAL WORLD is full of secrets and surprises, but how many of them do you know? With a series of intriguing questions, this section will test your knowledge of the Earth and its atmosphere, rocks and minerals, and the amazing lives of plants and animals. See if you can answer the questions here, then turn over the pages to see if you were right.

Which insect looks like a stick?

Why are fire salamanders black and yellow?

Which duck has "teeth"?

Which lion has a powerful sting?

Why are some flowers red?

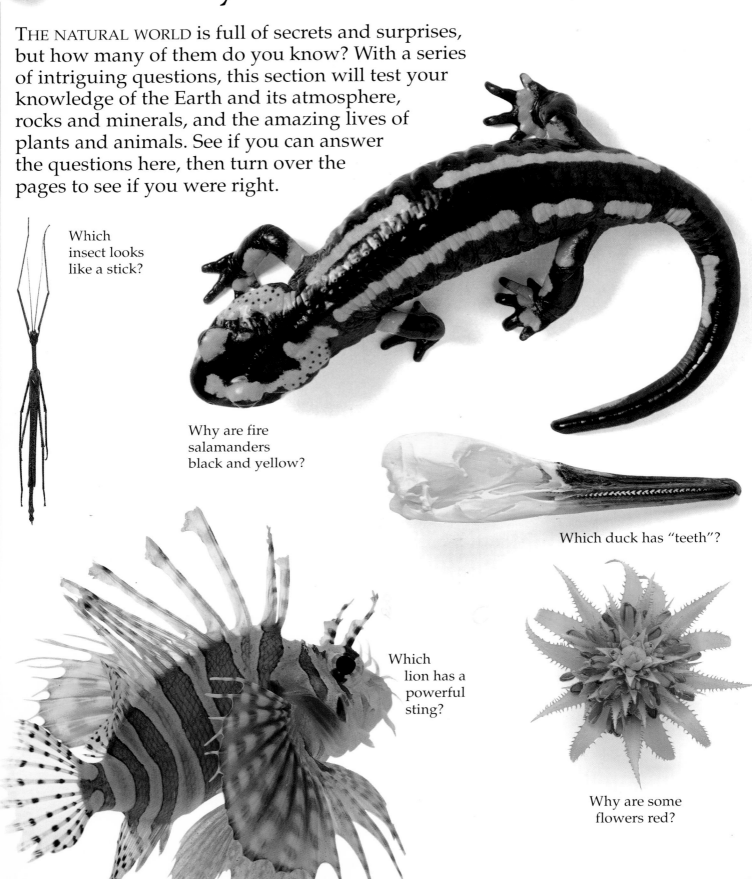

4

Who or what is an orrery?

How does the arrow-poison frog get its name?

How does a snake hatch?

What can a geologist learn from a shellfish called Nautilus?

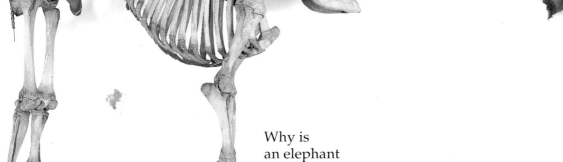

Why is an elephant like a bridge?

What makes some leaves turn red in autumn?

Why is the Earth unique?

THE EARTH is the only one of the nine planets in the solar system able to sustain life. Five of the other planets are simply balls of gas, and of the four remaining rocky planets – Mercury, Venus, Mars, and Earth – only Earth has the right kind of atmosphere. Earth's atmosphere not only contains the oxygen all living creatures need to breathe, but it also keeps the surface of the planet at just the right temperature, stopping it getting ferociously hot like Venus or icy cold like Mercury.

The Earth's thin, solid, outer layer, called the crust

Inner core of solid metal

Mantle, made of hot partly molten rock

Outer core of liquid metal

Q Why is the Earth like treacle sponge?

A The Earth may seem solid, but just below the thin crust is the mantle. The mantle is made of rock similar to the crust, but is so hot that in places it is melted into magma, like treacle in a treacle sponge. In fact, treacle is sometimes used in experiments to mimic the way magma behaves.

Air rises and cools

Air warms and dries as it moves down the far side of the range

Moist air

Rain on summit

Q Why do mountains have a wet and a dry side?

A Mountain ranges are often wet on the side facing the rain-bearing winds and dry on the other. When a moist air stream meets a mountain range, it is forced up towards the summit. As it rises it cools, causing the moisture to condense into thick, grey clouds which become saturated and fall as rain. As the cold air moves on down the far side of the mountain range, it gets warmer and dries out.

Wet *Dry*

Q Who invented thermometers?

A No-one knows for certain, but the famous Italian astronomer Galileo Galilei (1564–1642) was among the first to make one in Florence in 1593. The beautiful Florentine thermometer shown here dates from shortly after. Temperature changes are registered by the rise and fall of the glass balls in the water in the tubes.

Q How can you forecast the weather using a pine cone?

A Pine cones are among the most reliable of all natural weather indicators. In dry weather, the scales dry up and open out. If they start to close up, it is a sure sign that wet weather is on the way.

6

Q How many sides has a snowflake?

A In the late 19th century, American farmer Wilson W. Bentley photographed thousands of snowflakes under a microscope and never found two the same. But all snowflakes have six sides and are usually formed from flat, plate-like crystals, though occasionally the crystals may be needle- or rod-shaped. Outside the tropics, most rain starts as snow. Snow falls when the temperature of the air is just cold enough for the snow flakes to flutter to the ground before they melt. Sometimes, snow can be falling on the mountain tops while in the valley it is raining.

Q What is a mercury barometer?

A A barometer is a device for measuring atmospheric pressure. This is useful to know because a fall in pressure can indicate the onset of stormy weather and a rise in pressure goes with stable, clear weather. Mercury barometers show pressure by the changing level of liquid mercury in a glass tube. As air pressure rises, so it pushes the mercury higher up the tube; as it falls, the mercury drops. Mercury is used because it is the heaviest liquid known. A similar barometer filled with water instead would have to be over 10 m (32 ft) high.

Florentine barometer from around 1640

Head points into the wind, indicating the direction the wind is blowing from

The first weather cocks appeared on churches in the ninth century and were probably a reminder of the cock that crowed when St. Peter denied Christ three times

Q How can a cockerel tell you the weather?

A Winds from a particular direction usually bring a certain kind of weather – which is why people often have weathervanes to show where the wind is coming from. Many of these are in the shape of a cockerel. The cockerel sits on a cross showing north, east, south, and west.

Gnomon

Moon

Earth

Sun

Q Why did medieval sailors rely on a quadrant?

A A quadrant was a simple instrument in the shape of a quarter circle used by medieval sailors to measure the height of particular stars in the night sky. From this, they could calculate how far north or south they were. On this quadrant, the central dial can be rotated to show the positions of important constellations, such as the Great Bear, at different times of the year.

Brass sundial, 18th century

Q How can you tell the time from the position of the Sun?

A Using a sundial, it is possible to tell the time from the position and angle of the Sun. As the Sun appears to move across the sky during the day, so the shadow cast by the needle, or "gnomon", moves round the dial. The dial is marked to indicate the time wherever the shadow falls. Since the path of the Sun varies from place to place, sundials must be set up correctly for each place to give an accurate reading.

Q Who or what is an orrery?

A Once it became clear in the 1600s that the Earth circled around the Sun and not the Sun around the Earth, astronomers began to build clockwork models to show how the Earth and Moon moved during the course of a year. These devices are called orreries after Charles Boyle, Earl of Orrery (1676–1731) for whom the first one was made.

Q What was the biggest volcanic eruption in history?

A One of the best ways to tell the size of an eruption is to work out how much ash it blew out. On this basis, the biggest in history was that of Tambora in Indonesia in 1815, which blasted out some 80 cubic km of ash into the air, giving the world cool summers and cold winters for years after. When Mt. Pinatubo erupted in the Philippines in 1991, it blew out 7 cubic km.

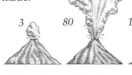

3	80	18	12	1	1
Vesuvius Italy A.D. 79	*Tambora Indonesia* 1815	*Krakatau Indonesia* 1883	*Katmai Alaska* 1912	*St. Helens USA* 1980	*El Chichón Mexico* 1982

7

How are rocks formed?

ALL ROCKS ARE FORMED in one of three ways: volcanic rocks form from molten rock within the Earth; sedimentary rocks form when the remains of rocks worn down by the weather are washed into the sea and deposited as sediments; and metamorphic rocks are rocks that have been transformed by the effect of heat and pressure inside the Earth.

White quartz

Vein of gold

Nautilus

Q Where does gold come from?

A Gold usually forms in veins along with quartz crystals in volcanic rocks. The veins were once cracks in the rock filled with hot, mineral-rich water. When the rock and the water cooled down, solid gold and quartz were left behind. Gold sometimes comes from veins like these, but may also be found as fine dust in rivers where it is washed down, as the rocks containing veins of gold are worn away by the weather.

Q Which rock is used to make blue paint?

A The blue paint pigment called azure was once made by crushing the copper mineral azurite.

Q What can a geologist learn from a shellfish called Nautilus?

A A geologist, or rock and mineral expert, can tell the age of sedimentary rocks from the range of fossils in them. Nautilus belongs to a class of sea creatures called cephalopods which first appeared 500,000,000 years ago. Over this time, 10,000 species have come and gone. Identifying species of fossilized cephalopods helps geologists pinpoint the age of the rock.

Q What is tiger's eye?

A Tiger's eye is a crystal made when veins of silk-blue asbestos crystals are dissolved by solutions which deposit quartz in their place. The quartz grows exactly in place of the tiny asbestos fibres.

Q What makes granite pink?

A Granite is one of the most common igneous rocks, made from crystals of quartz, feldspar, and mica. It turns pink when it contains a high proportion of potassium feldspar.

Q Which rock gives red paint?

A The pigment in vermilion red paint was once made by crushing the poisonous ore of mercury called cinnabar. The idea originated in China in prehistoric times and was introduced into Europe in the Middle Ages.

Cinnabar

Azurite

Q How does amethyst get its colour?

A Amethyst is a purple form of quartz. According to a 16th-century verse, Bacchus, the ancient Greek god of wine, declared in a rage that the first person he passed would be eaten by tigers. But when this person turned out to be the lovely maiden Amethyst, the goddess Diana turned her to stone to save her from the tigers. Regretting his anger, Bacchus poured red wine over the stone as an offering to Diana, turning the stone purple.

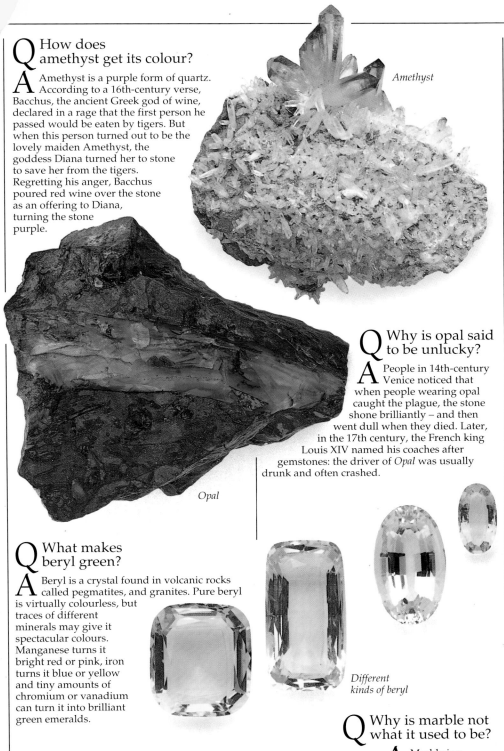

Amethyst

Opal

Q Why is opal said to be unlucky?

A People in 14th-century Venice noticed that when people wearing opal caught the plague, the stone shone brilliantly – and then went dull when they died. Later, in the 17th century, the French king Louis XIV named his coaches after gemstones: the driver of *Opal* was usually drunk and often crashed.

Q How are crystals thought to bring good health?

A Some people believe that crystals may be able to cure disease. They say that as light reflects off the crystals, the aura or electro-magnetic field of a person's body absorbs energy. This energy is thought to make the person more aware of the cause of the problem and helps to heal the body.

Q Why is ruby like sandpaper?

A Ruby is a form of the mineral corundum which is second only to diamond in hardness. Emery is another form of corundum. It is used in a fine form of sandpaper called emery paper, which electricians use to clean electrical contacts.

Different colours of corundum

Q What makes beryl green?

A Beryl is a crystal found in volcanic rocks called pegmatites, and granites. Pure beryl is virtually colourless, but traces of different minerals may give it spectacular colours. Manganese turns it bright red or pink, iron turns it blue or yellow and tiny amounts of chromium or vanadium can turn it into brilliant green emeralds.

Different kinds of beryl

Q Why do surgeons rely on diamonds?

A Diamond is the hardest substance in the world and so is used in many cutting and abrasive tools. Glaziers use pens with diamond tips to score a line on a sheet of glass to give a clean break. Besides being hard, diamond does not corrode, and so scalpels with diamond blades like the one shown here are often used for delicate surgical operations such as eye surgery.

Q Why is marble not what it used to be?

A Marble is a metamorphic rock, formed when limestone is transformed by the intense heat of a volcanic intrusion – that is, a volcanic upwelling which does not break through the Earth's surface. The smooth, lustrous stone has been popular since ancient Greek times and was used to make the frieze of the Parthenon temple in Athens known as the Elgin marbles.

Q What does jade mean?

A The Spanish conquerors of Mexico believed the green stones carved by the native people could cure kidney complaints. They called them kidney stones or *piedra de ijada* from which the word jade derives. Jade is a greenish-white rock found as either nephrite or jadeite. It has been treasured in China for over 2,000 years.

9

Why are plants green?

ANIMALS MUST FIND AND EAT OTHER LIVING THINGS to survive, but plants can make their own food by absorbing sunlight in a process called photosynthesis. This gives the plant the energy to change carbon dioxide in the air and minerals in water into food. Photosynthesis depends on special organs called chloroplasts inside leaf cells. Chloroplasts contain a green substance called chlorophyll, and it is this that makes plants green.

Sepal

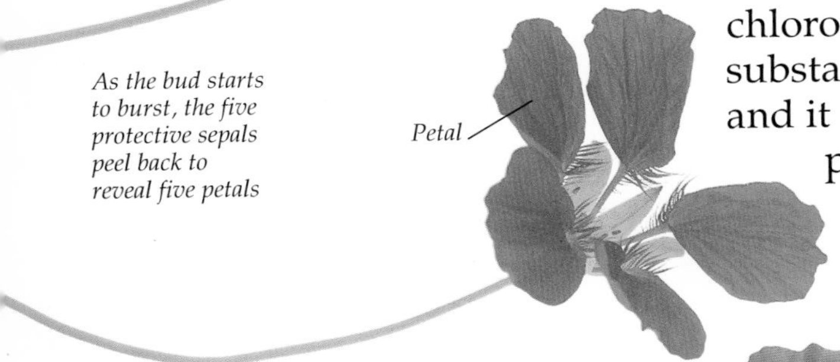

As the bud starts to burst, the five protective sepals peel back to reveal five petals

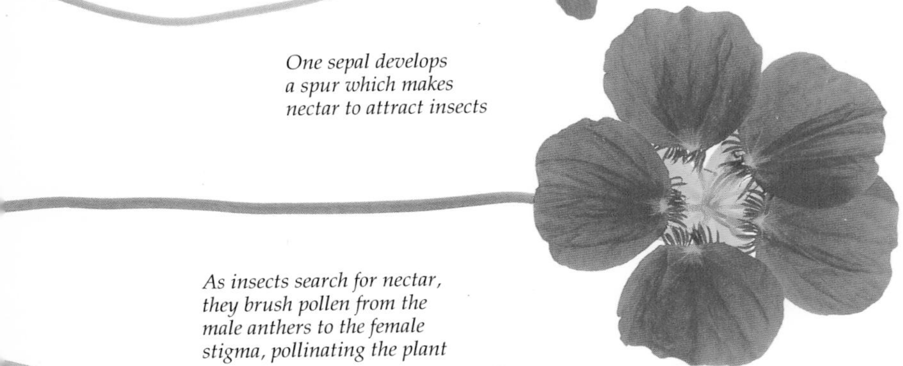

Petal

One sepal develops a spur which makes nectar to attract insects

As insects search for nectar, they brush pollen from the male anthers to the female stigma, pollinating the plant

Garden nasturtium

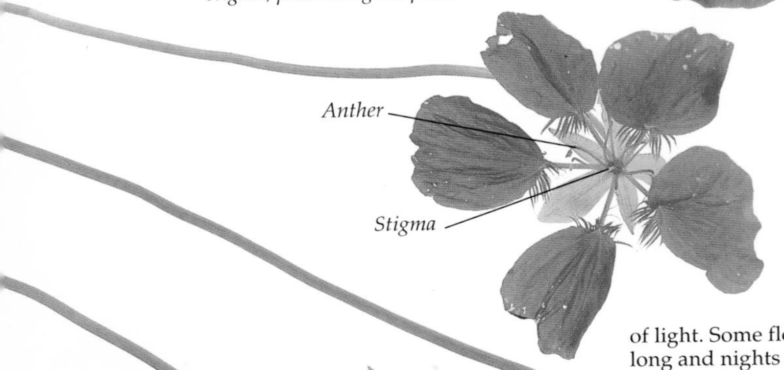

Anther

Stigma

After a few days, the petals shrivel

The flower makes three seeds inside a fruit

Gold head decoration from ancient Greece

Liverwort

Lid

Q What makes a plant flower?

A All flowering plants have a mechanism to ensure their blooms develop at just the right time of year. Most respond to the amount of light. Some flower only when days are long and nights are short; others flower only when nights are long and days are short, which is why chrysanthemums will never flower if lit at night by artificial light. The garden nasturtium shown here belongs to a family of plants from South America; it flowers only in mid summer, when the light is sufficient.

Q How did Greek athletes earn their laurels?

A Winners at the Pythian games in ancient Greece were crowned with the entwined twigs of the laurel tree. The laurel was sacred to the god Apollo, who was the patron of all athletes. The Romans adopted the custom and crowned victorious generals with laurel wreaths. Gold laurel wreaths were worn by Roman emperors instead of crowns.

Q Do all plants have flowers?

A No, not all. Most plants – 250,000 different kinds – are indeed flowering plants or angiosperms, including everything from roses to oak trees. But there are 500 or so gymnosperms – that is, conifers and cycads – which make their seeds in cones, not flowers. There are also plants that grow not from seeds but spores, including fungi, lichen, mosses, ferns and liverworts.

Q Which plants drown insects ?

A At the ends of the leaves of the insect-eating pitcher plant are traps shaped like jugs or pitchers, with a lid to keep out rain. Insects are lured to the pitcher by sweet nectar produced around the slippery rim. When an insect lands on the rim, it slips inside, and drowns in the fluid at the bottom.

Q When did the first flowers bloom?

A Mosses and fungi probably appeared some 400 million years ago, and by 300 million years ago, there were vast forests of huge cycads and giant ferns. But the first flowering plants did not appear until the middle of the Cretaceous period 100 million years or so ago, in the heyday of the dinosaurs.

Magnolias are among the oldest of all flowering plants, appearing 100 million years ago

Q Why are some flowers red?

A Flowers pollinated by birds are often bright red because the bright colour attracts the birds. The urn plant shown here grows high up on trees, so must be especially bright to attract birds. Flowers pollinated by insects, however, are rarely red, because insects, except for butterflies, cannot see red.

A shoot appears, then the first leaves

Q Is a pepper a fruit or a vegetable?

A Most of the plants we eat are either fruits or vegetables. Every flowering plant has a fruit. The fruit contains the seed from which a new plant will grow. Fruits come in many shapes, sizes and colours, from blackcurrants, to oranges, bananas and tomatoes. Peppers are true fruits, because they are formed from the ovary (egg-sac) of the pepper flower and nothing else.

Q What is a seed?

A A seed contains all that is needed for a new plant to grow. It holds the embryo, from which the seedling develops. It also holds enough food to sustain the growing plant through germination (the first stages of growth), either packed around the embryo or stored in special internal leaves called cotyledons.

A seed grows a single root

Once the leaves appear, the plant can make its own food by photosynthesis

A damselfly lands on the trap and touches the trigger bristles

Special cells filled with liquid make the jaw snap shut on the fly in less than two fifths of a second

Q Which plants snap to catch their food?

A Venus' flytraps are amazing insect-eating plants with leaves that look like a safe landing place for any unwary insect. But they are far from safe. The moment an insect brushes the sensitive hairs on the leaf surface, they snap shut in a fraction of a second like a pair of jaws.

After half an hour, the trap closes fully and the plant begins to digest its prisoner with acids and other chemicals

11

How high are the world's tallest trees?

THE TALLEST TREES OF ALL are the wellingtonias or giant sequoias of California, which grow hundreds of metres tall and can weigh more than 6,000 tonnes. The smallest trees, however, may be only a few centimetres high. Sequoias are conifers, which have narrow, hard leaves known as scales or needles. The other two main kinds of trees are broadleaved trees, with broad, flat leaves, and tropical palms.

New bark

Bark

Young tree

Mature tree

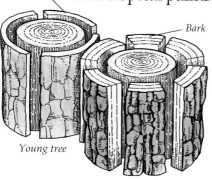

Q How does a tree grow?

A A tree can get taller and spread wider as cells at the tip of each twig divide to make the twig longer. The trunk and branches grow fatter as cells divide in a layer called the cambium, just below the bark.

Q What grows from a little acorn?

A A tall oak tree. The acorn is the fruit of the oak tree and contains its seed. In a good year, a single oak tree produces over 50,000 acorns. Most are eaten by animals, but a few survive to grow into trees the following spring.

Cinchona bark

Q What bark is better than a bite?

A The bite of a mosquito can give you malaria, but this disease can be treated with a chemical called quinine, extracted from the bark of the Peruvian cinchona tree. Aspirin is another drug based on chemicals from tree bark – this time the willow tree. The chemical name for aspirin-like drugs, *salicylates*, comes from the Latin name for the willow, *salix*.

Ripe Victoria plums

Q What would you do with a drupe?

A Eat it! A drupe is a kind of fruit that grows on certain trees, such as Victoria plums, cherries, and walnuts. Drupes are just like any other fruit, except that there are no pips, just a single hard stone containing the seed.

Q How did trees replace reeds?

A When the Egyptians wrote their amazing hieroglyphic script over 5,000 years ago, they used sharpened reed pens on paper made from strips of the papyrus reed that used to grow along the Nile. Nowadays, although the word "paper" comes from papyrus, the paper we write on is nearly always made from pulped wood fibre. And instead of a reed pen, you would probably use a wooden pencil.

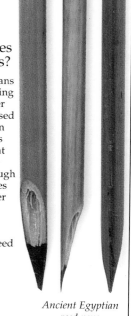

Ancient Egyptian reed pens

Q How can you tell the age of a tree?

A Trees grow for only a short period each year, and the rings show the amount the cambium has grown in each year. In a mature tree, the cambium typically grows 2.5 cm (1 in) a year, so the rings are 2.5 cm (1 in) wide, but they may be thinner for bad years. By counting the number of rings, you can tell how old a tree is.

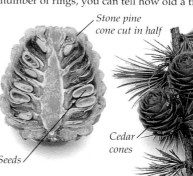

Stone pine cone cut in half

Seeds

Cedar cones

Q Why do conifers have cones?

A Unlike other trees, conifers do not have flowers. The seed develops inside a cone instead. When cones first appear on the tree, they are soft and green and little bigger than a pea. Only after they are pollinated do they grow big and turn brown and hard. Once this happens, a seed gradually develops beneath each of the cone's scales. When it is ripe, the cone breaks up to release the seeds.

Q What is a deciduous tree?

A Deciduous trees are trees that shed their leaves every year. Before the leaves die and fall off, they often turn brilliant reds, oranges and yellows.

Q What makes some leaves turn red in autumn?

A As the days get shorter and colder, the green pigment in the leaves breaks down, allowing other red, blue, or yellow pigments to shine through. The result is often a brilliant burst of colour before the leaves fall off and die.

Leaves of the deciduous European oak

Q Which trees are wooden rowing boats made from?

A Unlike the big sailing ships of the past, which were often made of tough but costly woods such as oak, rowing boats are generally made from less valuable woods such as larch. For the boat's hull the wood is cut into flat planks or strakes. It is then softened inside a steam-filled box and bent into the right curved shape. Once bent, the strakes are secured to the boat's inner framework.

Q Why are rowan berries red?

A To help scatter the rowan tree's seeds. Inside every berry is a seed from which a new rowan tree could grow. Birds such as thrushes, fieldfares and blackbirds are attracted by the bright red and eat the berries. But the hard seeds pass through their system undigested, and so the birds help scatter the seeds far and wide.

Catalpa leaf

Q Which deciduous tree has the biggest leaves?

A Catalpas or Indian bean trees have leaves that reach a giant 30 cm (1 ft) or more in length in the space of a single growing season. Of course, evergreen leaves can grow much bigger than deciduous leaves because evergreen trees do not lose their leaves every year. Banana leaves, for instance, can grow to several metres.

Mature catalpa tree

Q Who made bark boats?

A The paper-like bark of birch trees is so light and tough that the natives of North America used it for making canoes. These canoes were even light enough to carry overland to avoid rapids.

13

Why are some animals poisonous?

SOME ANIMALS AND PLANTS just happen to be poisonous to eat – like laburnum seeds, which birds can eat without any ill effects, but which can cause convulsions and death in humans. A few creatures use poison to stun or kill prey. But for many animals and plants, poison is vital for safety – a last line of defence against predators. Most mammals and birds, however, do not have poisons, and must defend themselves in other ways.

Running right down the middle of every spine is a venom gland

Q Why is an arrow-poison frog like an African leaf beetle?

A They both have a poison used by hunters. South African bush people smear the poison from the leaf beetle on their arrows to kill their prey quickly. The indigenous peoples of South and Central America do the same with the deadly poison exuded by the skin glands of the brilliantly coloured arrow-poison frog shown here. They collect the poison by holding the frog over a fire. As the frog sweats, the poison is scraped from its skin into a jar. The poison can quickly kill a person. There is a frog even more poisonous than the arrow-poison frog, though. The kokoi makes a poison called batrachotoxin. Just 0.0001 g of it can kill a human.

Q Which lion has a powerful sting?

A The tropical lionfish – also known as the firefish, scorpionfish or dragonfish – is beautiful but deadly. Each of the 13 spines on its back, the two on its jaw and the three beneath its tail are tipped with glands that ooze one of the most powerful of all venoms.

Q Which snake can kill an elephant?

A The king cobra is the biggest of all poisonous snakes, growing over 4 m (13 ft) long. When disturbed it lifts its head and strikes its fangs straight through the victim's skin. A single bite can kill an elephant in four hours.

Armadillo

Q Why doesn't an armadillo need poison?

A Because it has a hard shell like a suit of armour, made from overlapping plates of bone covered with scales. If threatened, the three-banded armadillo can quickly curl up into a tight, almost impenetrable, ball.

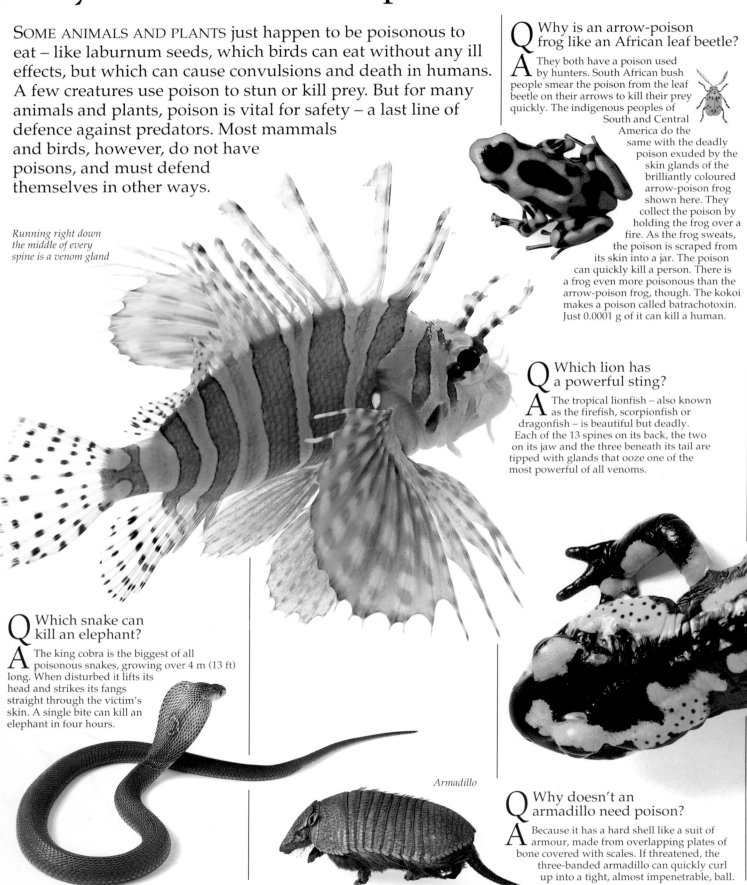

Snakelocks sea anemone

Q Which fishes blow themselves up like a balloon?

A Porcupine fish and pufferfish look like normal fish most of the time, but when threatened with danger, they can swallow water which inflates them into a ball two or three times their usual size. This not only startles predators but makes them difficult to swallow. When danger is past, the fish slowly deflates again.

Pufferfish

Q Why shouldn't you pick flowers or eat jelly in the sea?

A Because most sea flowers are anemones and jellies are jellyfish. These sea creatures, called coelenterates, cannot move fast to catch prey or avoid attack but have tiny, sensitive cells in their tentacles which can give a nasty sting.

Ferocactus

Q Why is a cactus so prickly?

A Cacti are plants of the deserts of the Americas and survive in the parched conditions by storing moisture in their thick, almost waterproof stems. The sharp spines protect them not only from attack by animals, but probably also from heat and cold.

Q Why should you beware of female hornets?

A Because they have the most painful stings of the wasp family. The sting is an adaptation of the egg-laying ovipositor.

Q What is the world's sleepiest mammal?

A The western European hedgehog spends most of its life asleep. During the summer it sleeps 18 hours day, only waking up a few times at night to forage for food. In winter, it sleeps all the time. It is quite safe when it is asleep, though, for it curls up into an uneatable prickly ball. Only sloths, armadillos and opossums sleep as long.

Q What do spiders do with their victims?

A Most spiders stun or kill their victims ready for eating with a bite from their poisonous jaws. Although a spider bite can be painful, however, few spiders are dangerous to humans – even the giant bird-eating tarantulas. One real exception is the quite small female black widow spider, whose bite can kill a child.

Q Why are fire salamanders black and yellow?

A To warn potential attackers that they are poisonous to eat. In the natural world, the colours black and yellow are often a sign that an animal is poisonous or has an unpleasant taste. Many wasps and hornets have black and yellow stripes as a warning to enemies that they have a painful sting.

Tarantula from Sri Lanka

15

Why are polar bears white?

BECAUSE POLAR BEARS ARE WHITE they blend in with the snow and ice of the Arctic landscape in which they live. Many animals use camouflage like this to remain hidden against their background – a huge advantage to both hunter and hunted alike. But not all animals rely on blending in with their background to avoid being eaten. Some scare off any would-be predators with bright colours, while others simply pretend they are something else such as a plant, or a more deadly, poisonous animal.

The Sinaloan milk snake is harmless to humans

Indian leaf butterfly

Citrus swallowtail butterfly chrysalis

Chameleon

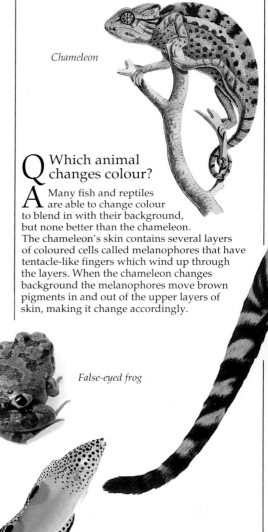

Q What is the difference between a coral snake and a milk snake?

A The coral snake has red stripes bordered by yellow and is highly venomous while the milk snake has red stripes bordered by black and is harmless. So predators are unlikely to attack the milk snake in case it turns out to be a coral snake. An old rhyme goes: "Red to yellow, kill a fellow; red to black, venom lack." Milk snakes were once thought to steal milk from cowsheds.

Q Which insect looks like a stick?

A Stick insects are so long and slender they look just like sticks. They avoid attack by hanging almost motionless in shrubs looking like dead twigs.

Stick insect

Hover-fly

Q Which fly spends its life looking like a wasp?

A This hover-fly, with its striped black-and-yellow jacket, looks just like a wasp, but it has no sting and is quite harmless. Most animals are scared off by the disguise and leave the fly alone.

Q When does a butterfly look like a dead leaf?

A When it is an Indian leaf butterfly. It has one of the most deceptive natural disguises. At rest, with its leaves folded, it looks remarkably like an old leaf on a stem. When it lies on the ground among leaf litter, it is almost totally invisible. Many insects mimic leaves during their vulnerable chrysalis stage.

False-eyed frog

Q Why do some creatures have "eyes" on their backs?

A The *Taenaris macrops* butterfly of New Guinea has two huge eyespots on its rear wings. If it is threatened by a predator while feeding on its favourite banana leaves, it flashes the two eyespots to startle the attacker off. Certain frogs and fish such as the twinspot wrasse have similar eyespots.

Q Which animal changes colour?

A Many fish and reptiles are able to change colour to blend in with their background, but none better than the chameleon. The chameleon's skin contains several layers of coloured cells called melanophores that have tentacle-like fingers which wind up through the layers. When the chameleon changes background the melanophores move brown pigments in and out of the upper layers of skin, making it change accordingly.

Twinspot wrasse

Q Which beetle mimics a seed?

A The ground-living tenebrionid beetle of Western Australia cannot easily be spotted by predators because it looks just like a seed.

Decorator crab

Q Why does a plaice have both eyes on one side of its body?

A So it can still see when it is lying flat on the sea bed. The plaice is a flatfish which spends most of its life at the bottom of the ocean. Although it starts life like any other fish, with one eye on either side of its body, as it grows older the left eye gradually moves around the head to join the right. After only three weeks, both eyes are on the camouflaged righthand side of the body and the lefthand side remains white and blind. Like other flatfish, a plaice is able to change the pattern and colour of the skin on the upper side of its body to suit the pattern and colour of the sea bed.

Q Why are some crabs like Christmas trees?

A Because they are festooned with decorations. The decorator crab adorns itself with all kinds of sea debris, such as shells and weed, so it avoids being spotted by predators.

Q Why are tigers striped?

A Tigers usually hunt alone at night among the trees, silently stalking prey such as antelope, deer and pigs, then pouncing from a few yards away. The dark stripes of their yellow fur break up their outline and so their victims cannot see them lurking in the shadows of the forest.

Q When do humans wear camouflage?

A Nearly all the time. Most clothes and hairstyles are designed to make the human body look more attractive, or hide its true form. Some people wear jackets with shoulder pads to make them look more impressive, or high-heeled shoes to make them look taller. In the 1880s, women wore a bustle under their skirts to make their hips wider, and a tight corset for a narrow waist and fuller bosom.

17

What do bones do?

BONES ARE THE RODS AND PLATES that make up a creature's skeleton. Skeletons range greatly in shape and size, from tiny hummingbirds to massive blue whales. But they all provide a rigid, protective framework for the body; the spine is the body's main support; the skull houses and protects the brain and the vulnerable eyes and ears; and the ribs form a protective cage around the heart and lungs.

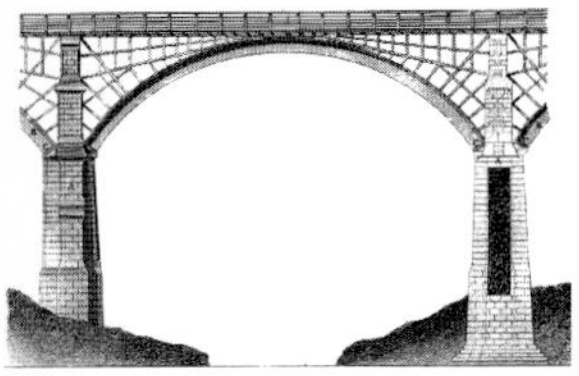

Arched bridges work in the same way as an elephant's skeleton

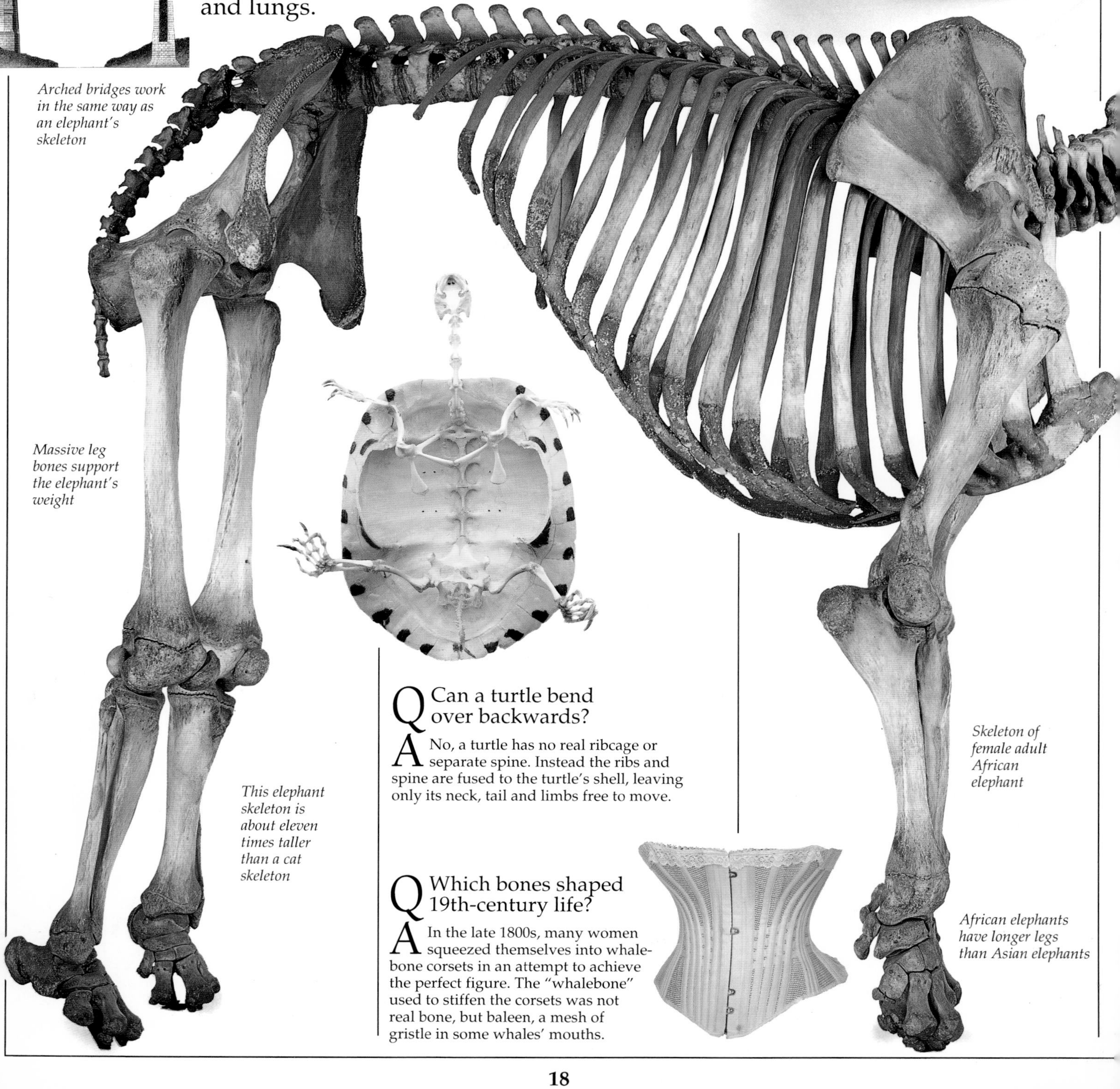

Massive leg bones support the elephant's weight

This elephant skeleton is about eleven times taller than a cat skeleton

Q **Which duck has "teeth"?**

A Unlike mammals and reptiles, birds do not have true teeth, which are made of bone. But mergansers, which are a kind of duck, have tooth-like serrations on the sides of their beak. They use their beak "teeth" to catch fish in fresh water and at sea.

"Teeth" are made of the same horny material as the beak

Q **Can a turtle bend over backwards?**

A No, a turtle has no real ribcage or separate spine. Instead the ribs and spine are fused to the turtle's shell, leaving only its neck, tail and limbs free to move.

Q **Which bones shaped 19th-century life?**

A In the late 1800s, many women squeezed themselves into whale-bone corsets in an attempt to achieve the perfect figure. The "whalebone" used to stiffen the corsets was not real bone, but baleen, a mesh of gristle in some whales' mouths.

Skeleton of female adult African elephant

African elephants have longer legs than Asian elephants

18

Australopithecus, 4–1 million years ago

Homo erectus, 1,500,000–300,000 years ago

Neanderthal 100,000–35,000 years ago

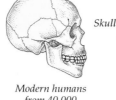
Modern humans from 40,000 years ago

Q How have human skulls changed?

A Over the past 2 million years, human skulls have gradually got a flatter face, smaller teeth, a less prominent jaw, and the top of the skull has become bigger and rounder to house the larger brain.

Q How many bones are there in the human body?

A Just over 200. They include 12 vertebrae (backbones), 24 ribs and a three-part breastbone, besides three large bones in each limb. Each hand has 27 bones, with eight wrist bones to allow them to swivel in almost any direction. Each hip consists of three bones fused together. They are rounded and so allow us to walk upright.

Skull

Vertebrae

Ribs

Sternum (breastbone)

Radius

Ulna

Ilium

Sacrum

Cocccyx

Pubis

Ischium

Femur

Fibula

Tibia

Metatarsals

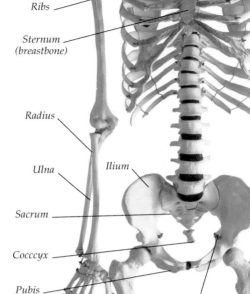

Bullfrog skeleton

Q Why are frogs such good jumpers?

A The frog has one of the shortest spines of all, with only eight or nine vertebrae, so it is well adapted to stand the stresses of jumping. It also has long legs, with the thigh, calf, and foot all much the same length. As a frog jumps, each part of the leg straightens in turn, enabling the frog to leap huge distances.

Q Why is an elephant's skeleton like a bridge?

A Elephants, stone bridges and arches all work on the same mechanical principle, and so have a similar design. They all share the weight of their load between their supports. The load-bearing part curves upward in the middle to give extra strength.

Q Does a car have a skeleton?

A They used to. Old cars had a rigid internal skeleton called a chassis. Today, most cars have a body shell, not a chassis. But trucks and other large vehicles are still built on chassis. A whole range of different bodies can be bolted onto a truck chassis.

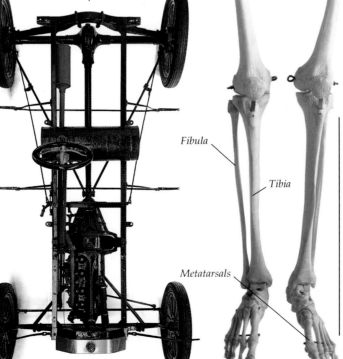

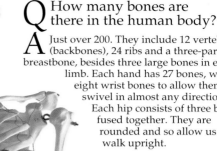
Stag beetle

Wood-boring beetle

Q Which creatures have skeletons on the outside?

A Insects, spiders and shellfish all have a hard outer casing, or exoskeleton, rather than bones. Like an internal skeleton, this exoskeleton provides support and protection, but it cannot expand. So the creature grows by moulting its exoskeleton every now and then and growing a new one. Above a certain size the exoskeleton becomes too thick and heavy to be moulted, which is why animals with exoskeletons tend to be small.

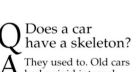

What makes a home?

A HOME IS A PLACE OF SHELTER – from the weather, to hide from enemies, or to bring young safely into the world. For some animals it is just a crack in a tree or a hole in the ground. But many small creatures build burrows and nests. Rabbits and prairie dogs dig elaborate burrows in the ground. Birds and rodents build nests using anything from straw to old bottles. Termites build homes as elaborate in their way as a modern tower block.

Termite nest

Section through a South American paper wasps' nest

Common wasps' nest

Q Which insects live in multi-storey pagodas?

A In damp African rainforests, the ground is often so sodden that *Cubitermes* termites build their nest on a tall column to keep it dry. Each level has a sloping roof which sheds rain.

Q Who really invented papier mâché?

A South American paper wasps have made papier mâché nests for millions of years, chewing plant fibres into a papery pulp that hardens as it dries. The result is a material both light and strong, which they use to build huge hanging nests up to 1.8 m (6 ft) across.

Q How does a bird know how to build its nest?

A Birds rarely live in their nests all the time, but build them to rear their young. Experiments show nest building is instinctive, inherited as reliably as plumage and feeding habits. But each bird improves with practice, building at first rather crudely, but getting better with each season.

When a hermit crab is moving about, its head, antennae (feelers), front claws and first two pairs of legs are exposed

Q Where do squirrels live in winter?

A Like many rodents, the grey squirrel is a nest-builder. A squirrel's drey, or nest, is made in autumn high in a tree from materials such as leaves, straw, feathers, and even old newspapers. The squirrel sleeps here at night or shelters in bad weather.

Squirrel's drey

Beaver

Q Which animals are the best engineers?

A Beavers build elaborate lodges from mud and sticks, with a safe underwater entrance. They also erect sturdy dams in streams to keep the lodge entrance submerged. One beaver dam on the Jefferson River in the USA is 700 m (2,300 ft) long, and can bear the weight of a horse. When building a dam, a beaver may spend a long time selecting the right tree, gnawing through it with its sharp incisors, in just the right place to make it fall where the beaver wants it.

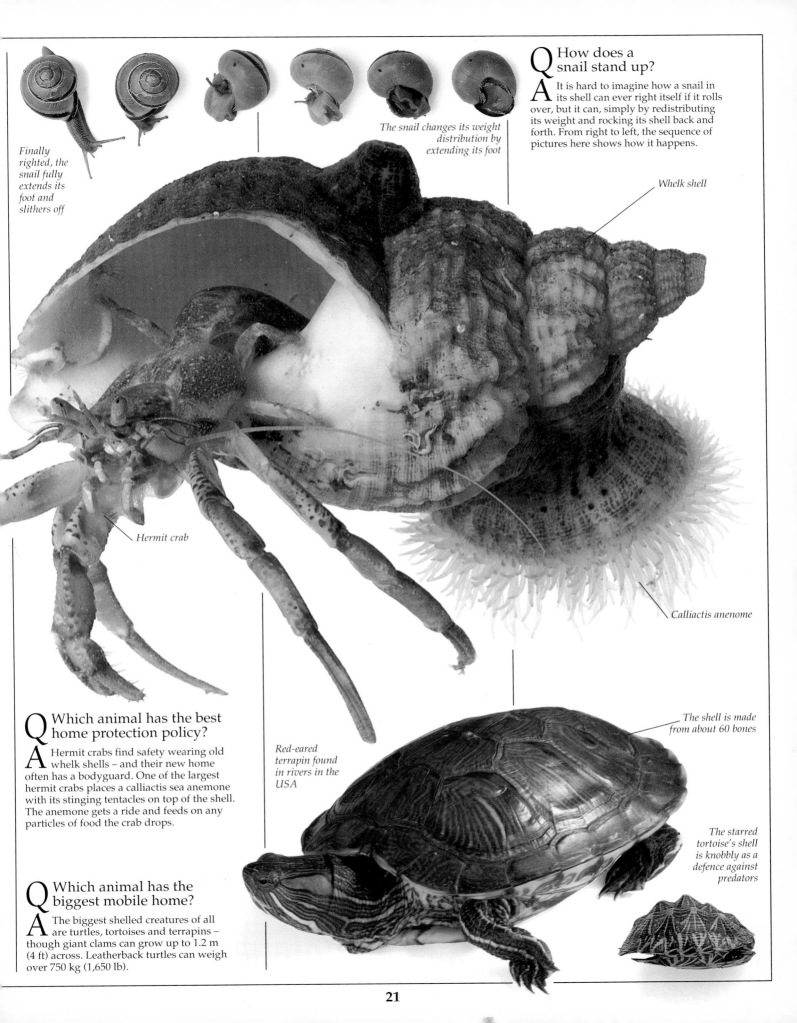

Finally righted, the snail fully extends its foot and slithers off

The snail changes its weight distribution by extending its foot

Q How does a snail stand up?

A It is hard to imagine how a snail in its shell can ever right itself if it rolls over, but it can, simply by redistributing its weight and rocking its shell back and forth. From right to left, the sequence of pictures here shows how it happens.

Whelk shell

Hermit crab

Calliactis anenome

Q Which animal has the best home protection policy?

A Hermit crabs find safety wearing old whelk shells – and their new home often has a bodyguard. One of the largest hermit crabs places a calliactis sea anemone with its stinging tentacles on top of the shell. The anemone gets a ride and feeds on any particles of food the crab drops.

Red-eared terrapin found in rivers in the USA

The shell is made from about 60 bones

The starred tortoise's shell is knobbly as a defence against predators

Q Which animal has the biggest mobile home?

A The biggest shelled creatures of all are turtles, tortoises and terrapins – though giant clams can grow up to 1.2 m (4 ft) across. Leatherback turtles can weigh over 750 kg (1,650 lb).

Who lays eggs?

NEARLY EVERY CREATURE starts life as an egg – even humans. Only creatures that reproduce asexually such as flatworms and hydra begin life any other way. But though most insects, birds, fish, reptiles and amphibians actually lay eggs, only a few mammals do, such as the duck-billed platypus of Australia. Most mammals and a few lizards and snakes are viviparous. This means they give birth to fully developed young.

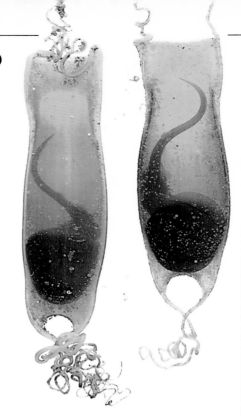

Male midwife toad from western Europe carrying strings of eggs on its back

Q What is a mermaid's purse?

A Mermaid's purses are the hard, horny egg cases of dogfish, skates and rays. A female dogfish usually lays them in pairs and attaches them to seaweeds by the long, curly tendrils at each corner. The embryos then grow by themselves for six to nine months before wriggling out into the water.

Q What makes a baby spiny anteater special?

A Spiny anteaters are monotremes, which means they are mammals that hatch from eggs. The only other monotremes are duckbilled platypuses.

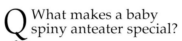

Q How does a young snake hatch out of its egg?

A A baby snake is ready to hatch from its egg at between seven and 15 weeks. To cut its way through the shell it has a special sharp egg tooth. Snake eggs vary considerably. Most are round and have a tough papery skin but some hardly look like eggs at all. The mother snake usually buries her eggs in soil or rotting vegetation and then leaves them there to hatch out on their own.

Q Why are guillemot eggs pointed?

A Guillemots are sea birds that lay their eggs on a bare cliff ledge rather than building a nest. The eggs' pointed shape probably saves the mother from accidentally knocking them off the ledge. Should the eggs begin to roll, their shape means they will roll right round in a circle.

Some males take on two or even three egg clutches

Eggs

Young larva

Mature larva

Q How does a stag beetle change as it grows up?

A Like many insects, it goes through several changes or metamorphoses, starting life as an egg, hatching to a larva then changing through several larval stages to a pupa from which the adult emerges.

Male pupa

Female pupa

Q How long does a bird's egg take to hatch?

A Birds' eggs are surprisingly tough, and it can take a baby bird hours or even days of hard work to break through into the outside world. Typically, though, it takes around half-an-hour. The pheasant pictured here took 33 minutes from the moment when the first crack appeared.

Q How does the midwife toad get its name?

A Remarkably, it is not the mother midwife toad who looks after the eggs, but the father. After they have been laid, he winds strings of eggs around his back legs and carries them around with him, dipping his legs in pools and streams every now and then to keep the eggs damp. After about three weeks, he returns to water for the eggs to hatch.

Darker colour shows egg will soon hatch

Caterpillar cuts its way out with sharp jaws

Caterpillar emerges from shell

Emu

Kiwi

Q Who lays the biggest eggs?

A Some dinosaurs laid huge eggs of course, but the biggest birds' eggs are laid by giant flightless birds. The extinct "elephant bird" of Madagascar laid eggs weighing 12 kg (26 lb). But ostriches and emus lay large eggs too. An ostrich's egg may weigh up to 1.5 kg (3.3 lb) and an emu's 0.7 kg (1.5 lb). The kiwi is no bigger than a chicken, yet lays eggs of 0.45 kg (1 lb) – more than a quarter of the female's entire weight.

Q When does a butterfly egg change colour?

A Butterfly and moth eggs laid in autumn go into a resting stage called diapause in winter. When spring comes and the weather gets warmer, the eggs darken in colour as the tiny caterpillars get ready to emerge by biting their way through the shell.

23

When did it happen?

HISTORY is full of fascinating facts about how human life first arose, how primitive hunters and gatherers first settled down to farm, trade, and build towns, and how civilizations and societies slowly grew. But how many of them do you know? Read the questions here, then turn over the pages and check your answers.

Who invented the chronometer?

Who was Darius the Great?

Why did the Spanish go to America?

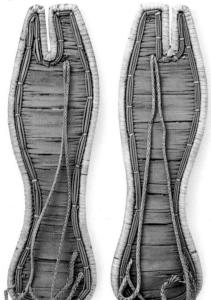

Who wore "paper" sandals?

Who made the first panpipes?

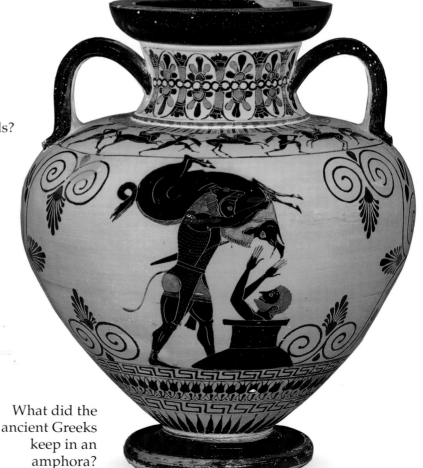

What did the ancient Greeks keep in an amphora?

How could you play a goblet?

24

Which beetle was sacred to the ancient Egyptians?

How did James Cook know where he was?

Who or what was an ammonite?

Who had tool-shaped coins?

Who were the first shepherd boys?

How did a 17th-century gentleman do up his baldric?

25

When did life begin?

THE EARTH IS ABOUT 4,600 MILLION YEARS OLD, but life probably began in the sea some 3,800 million years ago. Ancient rocks dating from this time contain microscopic specks which may be fossilized, bacteria-like organisms, and, in some 3,500-million-year-old rocks, there are ring-shaped fossils called stromatolites, a kind of algae which grew in warm, shallow seas. But it was not until 400 million years ago that the first primitive creatures walked on land.

Q **Who or what is an ammonite?**

A An ammonite is a kind of extinct shellfish that had a hard, external shell. Fossils of these creatures are very common in rocks dating from the time of the dinosaurs 200–64 million years ago. In northern England, people believed ammonites were the remains of coiled snakes turned to stone by the seventh-century abbess St. Hilda.

Fern

Cycad frond

Anthracite, the hardest form of coal

Q **How fast could a dinosaur run?**

A Studies of fossil feet and footprints prove that not all dinosaurs were cumbersome and slow. Some, especially the two-legged dinosaurs, may have been quite agile. The fossil foot here belonged to an *Iguanodon*, probably one of the slower two-legged dinosaurs, which could shuffle along at around 1.5 kmh (1 mph). Smaller, lighter dinosaurs may have been able to run at over 40 kmh (25 mph).

The shark Hybodus *appeared about 240 million years ago and grew to about 2.5 m (8 ft) long*

Q **When did sharks first terrorize the oceans?**

A The first sharks appeared in the ancient seas nearly 400 million years ago, which is about 200 million years before dinosaurs roamed the Earth. The remains of some of these early sharks were fossilized when they sank to the bottom of the sea. Hard parts such as spines or teeth fossilized more readily than soft parts such as the sharks' rubbery skeleton of cartilage.

Q **Why is coal called a fossil fuel?**

A Because it is made from the fossilized remains of giant ferns and cycads that grew in the steamy swamps that covered much of the world in the Carboniferous period, 345–280 million years ago. Oil and natural gas are also fossil fuels, but they are formed from the remains of sea creatures, not plants.

Q **Did dinosaurs eat flowers?**

A Many plant-eating dinosaurs would have eaten flowers, such as magnolias, which are among the oldest of all flowering plants. Still popular in gardens today, they date from around 100 million years ago.

Magnolia flower

Q **How old are sea urchins?**

A Sea urchins are among the oldest sea creatures and have lived in the oceans since at least the Cambrian period, some 490 million years ago. Because their skeletons or shells are made from a resistant substance called calcite, they are often preserved as fossils. Fossilized sea urchins are sometimes called thunderstones because people believed they had fallen from the sky during a thunderstorm.

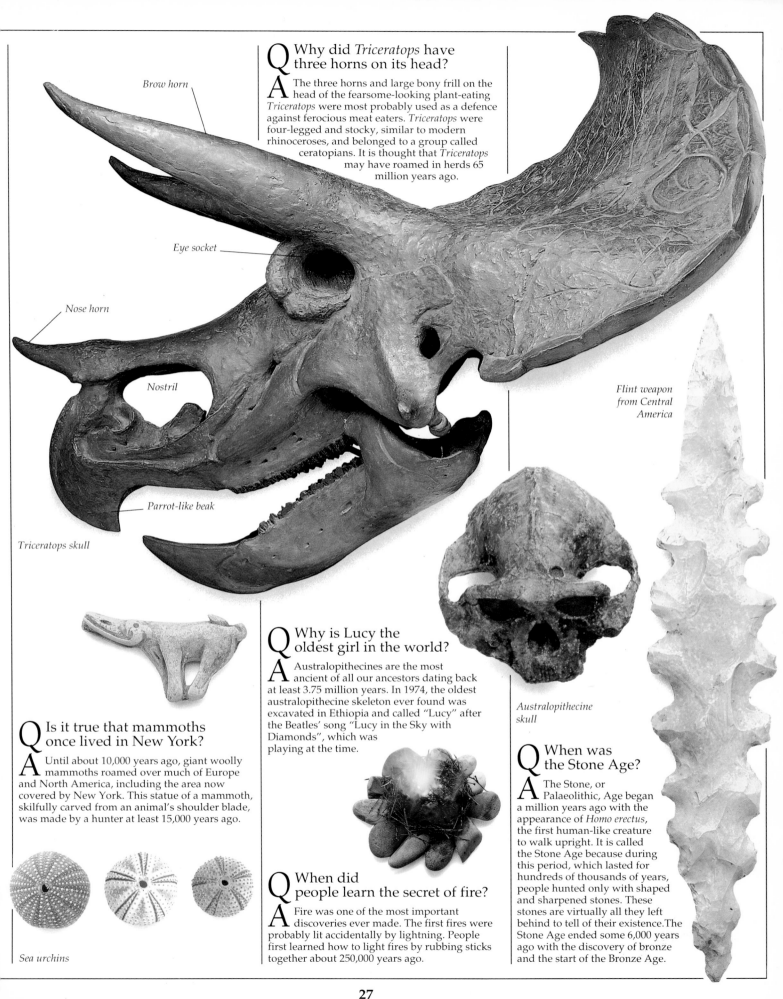

Q Why did *Triceratops* have three horns on its head?

A The three horns and large bony frill on the head of the fearsome-looking plant-eating *Triceratops* were most probably used as a defence against ferocious meat eaters. *Triceratops* were four-legged and stocky, similar to modern rhinoceroses, and belonged to a group called ceratopians. It is thought that *Triceratops* may have roamed in herds 65 million years ago.

Brow horn

Eye socket

Nose horn

Nostril

Parrot-like beak

Triceratops skull

Flint weapon from Central America

Q Why is Lucy the oldest girl in the world?

A Australopithecines are the most ancient of all our ancestors dating back at least 3.75 million years. In 1974, the oldest australopithecine skeleton ever found was excavated in Ethiopia and called "Lucy" after the Beatles' song "Lucy in the Sky with Diamonds", which was playing at the time.

Australopithecine skull

Q Is it true that mammoths once lived in New York?

A Until about 10,000 years ago, giant woolly mammoths roamed over much of Europe and North America, including the area now covered by New York. This statue of a mammoth, skilfully carved from an animal's shoulder blade, was made by a hunter at least 15,000 years ago.

Sea urchins

Q When did people learn the secret of fire?

A Fire was one of the most important discoveries ever made. The first fires were probably lit accidentally by lightning. People first learned how to light fires by rubbing sticks together about 250,000 years ago.

Q When was the Stone Age?

A The Stone, or Palaeolithic, Age began a million years ago with the appearance of *Homo erectus*, the first human-like creature to walk upright. It is called the Stone Age because during this period, which lasted for hundreds of thousands of years, people hunted only with shaped and sharpened stones. These stones are virtually all they left behind to tell of their existence. The Stone Age ended some 6,000 years ago with the discovery of bronze and the start of the Bronze Age.

27

Where is the oldest town?

FOR MOST OF PREHISTORY, people were nomads, travelling from place to place to hunt animals and gather wild plants to eat. But around 10-12,000 years ago, some people began to settle down and farm the land. Soon after, some small communities grew into towns, and with towns came the first civilizations. The word "civilization" comes from the Latin for town. No-one knows for certain where civilization began, but it was probably in the Middle East, where the world's most ancient cities are to be found. The oldest is Jericho, in the Israeli-occupied West Bank. It is over 10,000 years old.

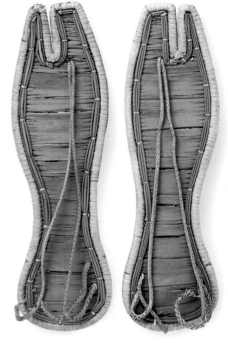

Q Why did Egyptians value Horus' eye?

A The "wedjat" eye symbolized the eye of the god Horus. It was torn out by Seth in the struggle for the throne of Egypt, but was magically restored. It was said to protect all who stood behind it.

Q Who invented eye-shadow?

A People have probably always painted their faces, but the first to wear anything like modern make-up were the Egyptians, over 4,000 years ago. Egyptian men and women both wore eye-paint, made from minerals ground on fine slate palettes.

Q Who wore "paper" sandals

A The Egyptians made a kind of paper for writing on, by cutting and flattening strips from the papyrus reed that once flourished along the river Nile. The word "paper" comes from papyrus. They also made sandals from papyrus, which were worn by people at all levels of society. Priests were forbidden to wear any other material on their feet.

Q Did early people play ball?

A Ancient Egyptian children played much the same games as children do today – including leapfrog, tug-of-war and skipping. They had balls made of clay filled with seed, which rattled as they were thrown.

Khnum

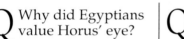

Q Which beetle was sacred to the ancient Egyptians?

A To the Egyptians the scarab, or dung beetle, symbolized the sun-God Khepri. They imagined Khepri pushed the Sun across the sky in the same way as the beetle pushes dung around.

Q Did Hapi make people happy?

A Hapi was the god of the river Nile's yearly flood. Ancient Egyptian farmers relied on the Nile flooding to irrigate their land and bring rich, fertile silt deposits, which benefitted their crops. Hapi would only rise in flood on the word of the ram-headed god Khnum, who ruled over the wild Nile cataracts. After the flood, happy farmers gave part of their crop to the god's temple in thanks.

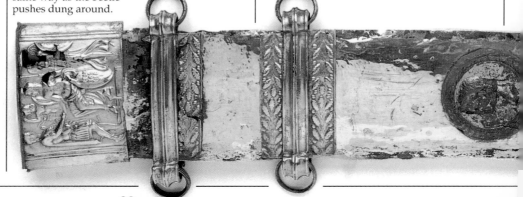

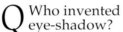

Q Who was Darius the Great?

A Darius the Great was King of Persia from 522 to 485 B.C. It was under him that the Persian Empire reached its greatest extent, stretching from Egypt to India. Darius divided the empire into regions or satrapies and founded the stunning city of Persepolis, which was an important civic and religious centre. This silver goat is just one of the treasures found near the remains of the city.

Q Who invented the signs of the zodiac?

A The first evidence of the signs of the zodiac comes from the ancient city of Babylon in what is now Iraq. Babylon was founded over 4,000 years ago and reached its height in the 18th century B.C. The Babylonian terracotta plaque here shows the ancestor of the water sign Aquarius carrying streams of water.

Q Which was the most powerful army in the ancient world?

A The Romans had the most powerful and disciplined army in the ancient world, and with it they built an empire that reached from Scotland to the Red Sea. The army played a very important role in Roman society and a talented soldier could expect promotion and rewards. This beautiful scabbard decorated with silver and gold may have been given to a Roman officer by the emperor Tiberius.

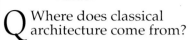

Q Where does classical architecture come from?

A Classical architecture is the style first seen in the beautiful temples of the ancient Greeks 2,500 years ago and widely imitated ever since. Greek temples were geometrical in shape with tall, graceful columns and broad horizontal lintels. Shown here is a roof tile from the temple to the god Apollo at Bassae in southern Greece.

Q What did the ancient Greeks keep in an amphora?

A The Greeks were famous for their high-quality pots made from clay fired to a rich reddish-brown. Pots were made in different shapes according to how they were used. Amphorae, like the pot shown here, were used for storing wine. Greek pottery was often beautifully decorated with scenes from Greek myths. In the early sixth century, potters used the black-figure technique, painting black figures on to red. Later they painted the background in black.

Q Did Romans have keys?

A Lock and keys are an ancient invention used by the Egyptians 4,000 years ago. The Romans, too, had locks and keys. Roman keys had a complicated shape which slotted through the keyhole into a pattern of holes in the hidden bolt.

29

Who believed in gods?

ALL ANCIENT CIVILIZATIONS had their own religions and beliefs. Most were polytheistic, which meant they worshipped more than one god. Much of what we know today comes to us through ancient myths or through archaeological finds that show the lives of the gods. Some of the best-known myths belong to the ancient Greeks.

Bronze head from eastern Turkey

Q Who was the ancient Greek goddess of love?

A Aphrodite, known to the Romans as Venus, was the ancient goddess of love. The word "aphrodisiac", meaning a love potion, comes from her name. She was said to have been born from the sea foam and blown by Zephyrs (West Winds) to Cyprus.

Ancient Greek vase painting from 460 B.C. showing Perseus and the Medusa

Q Why did the Egyptians mummify their dead?

A The Egyptians believed that a person's soul left the body at death. After the burial, the soul was reunited with the body. But, in order for the body and the soul to live on in the afterlife, the body had to be preserved by a mummification process known as embalming. This entailed cutting out the vital organs, then covering the body in crystals of natron, packing it with sawdust and leaves, and wrapping it in linen bandages. The mummified body was then laid in a coffin or mummy case. The technique of embalming developed gradually over ancient Egypt's long history. It reached its peak around 1000 B.C., but Romans living in Egypt were still being mummified in the third century A.D.

Q How many gods did the ancient Greeks have?

A The ancient Greeks had literally hundreds of gods. Besides scores of Olympian gods each with their own temple, there were many household and local gods attached to places, such as the river god shown in this fired clay face.

Q How did a mirror save Perseus?

A Perseus was a Greek hero sent to behead the terrible she-monster Medusa. But anyone who looked on the Medusa would turn to stone. To avoid this, and succeed in his task, Perseus looked only at her reflection in his shiny shield. In this picture, Medusa sinks to the ground as Perseus escapes with her head in his bag.

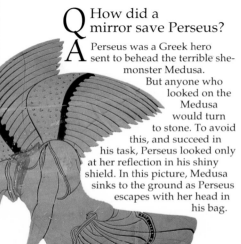

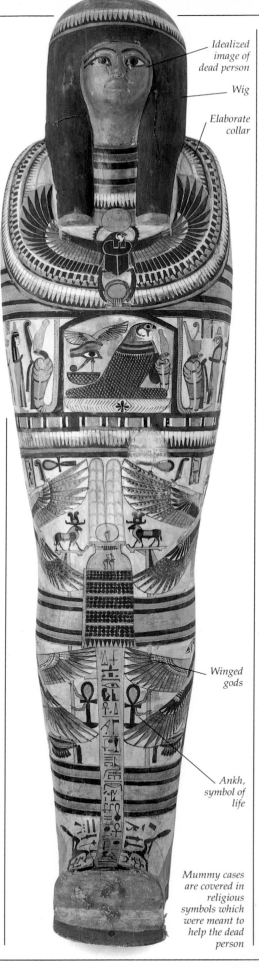

Idealized image of dead person

Wig

Elaborate collar

Winged gods

Ankh, symbol of life

Mummy cases are covered in religious symbols which were meant to help the dead person

Who was Horus and why was he important to the Egyptians?

Horus, represented by a falcon, was the Egyptian sky-god from whom all the pharaohs were descended. This royal bracelet depicts him as a child protected by two cobras.

What did the letters XP mean in ancient Rome?

For the ancient Romans, the letters XP were a sign of Christianity. X and P are symbols made from the first two letters of Christ's name in the Greek alphabet, *chi* (X) and *rho* (P). This fragment of gold glass from the last days of the Roman Empire shows a Christian family.

Who made this statue – and why?

This small, white marble statue of a female figure was made in ancient Greece probably about 2,500 years ago during the early Bronze Age. But people today still cannot be certain why it was made, or for whom. As it is of a stylized female figure, it may represent its owner or a goddess, or it may be a fertility symbol.

Who was the Babylonian goddess of love and war?

Ishtar was worshipped as the goddess of love and war by the Babylonians, Sumerians and Assyrians. She was the Babylonians' chief goddess, and the great blue northern gate of Babylon was named after her. This blue plaque comes from the temple of Ninurta in the Assyrian city of Nimrud and dates from around the ninth century B.C. The winged goddess is probably meant to represent Ishtar as goddess of love.

Who gave gold pendants to the gods?

These gold pendants were found in the Fosse Temple, a late Bronze-Age Canaanite sanctuary in the ancient Israeli city of Lachish. They were probably left there by Canaanite people as an offering to the gods.

Decoration formed when gold is beaten over a patterned object

What does the Jewish *menorah* represent?

Menorah is the Hebrew word for candlestick. In the Old Testament it refers to the seven-branched candlestick that stood in the Temple of Jerusalem and was removed by the Romans in A.D. 70.

Who was Pegasus?

Pegasus was the flying horse that sprung from the blood of the Medusa when Perseus cut off her head. He was given to the Greek hero Bellerophon to help him conquer the Chimera, a grotesque monster. But when Bellerophon tried to ride Pegasus to heaven, the horse was stung by a gadfly sent by Zeus and he was thrown back down to Earth.

Who were Zeus and Apollo and how were they related?

In ancient Greece, many of the gods and goddesses were related. Zeus was the king of all the gods and ruled the Earth and the sky. He is usually shown as a strong, bearded figure throwing a thunderbolt. Zeus had many children, one of whom was the handsome young Apollo. Apollo was the god of sunshine and of poetry, music and medicine.

Zeus

Apollo

31

Where is the Fertile Crescent?

FARMING BEGAN about 12,000 years ago in the Middle East. For the first time in human history, people began to form small communities, growing their own food and raising animals. As more and more settlements were gradually established, large areas of land were cultivated, and the whole region became known as the Fertile Crescent. Today, this area, which includes parts of modern-day Israel, Turkey, Iraq and Iran, is largely desert. But the farming techniques learned here have been adopted worldwide.

Pomegranate

Feathers were used to keep the arrow steady in the air

Fire-hardened wooden arrow

Flint-tipped arrow

Q What did early people eat?

A For thousands of years, people ate the animals and plants that they hunted and gathered. At first, animals were hunted by driving them into difficult ground and then beating them to death with stone axes. Later, sharp flint spears and arrows were used.

Q What were the first crops grown?

A The first crops were planted and harvested about 10,000 years ago. The first farmers in the Middle East grew barley and varieties of a cereal called einkorn shown here. Einkorn is a kind of wheat that grows wild in Turkey and Iran. By 5000 B.C, crop farmers in the Far East, India and South America were growing rice, oats, beans, peas and cassava.

Q When was the plough invented?

A In the early days of farming, farmers prepared the ground for seed with a hoe or a simple digging stick. By 3500 B.C., they were harnessing the sticks to oxen to make the first ploughs. Wooden ploughs wore out quickly, so in Europe in 500 B.C.they began to use iron ploughs similar to this one.

Q What fruit did early townspeople eat?

A People in the early civilizations of the Middle East ate almost as wide a variety of fruit as people there do now. Apples and dates were grown throughout the region by around 4000 B.C. Pomegranates were highly prized for their bitter-sweet juice and spread west from Asia Minor and Persia in around 2000 B.C.

Unleavened bread of the type made in the Stone Age

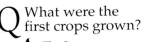

Q How did people make the first bread?

A The first bread was probably made from wild grasses long before wheat was cultivated. The first wheat bread was made 9,000 years ago. People beat the wheat to remove the grains, which were ground into flour on a big flat stone using a smaller rubbing stone. From the flour, they made unleavened bread (like pitta bread).

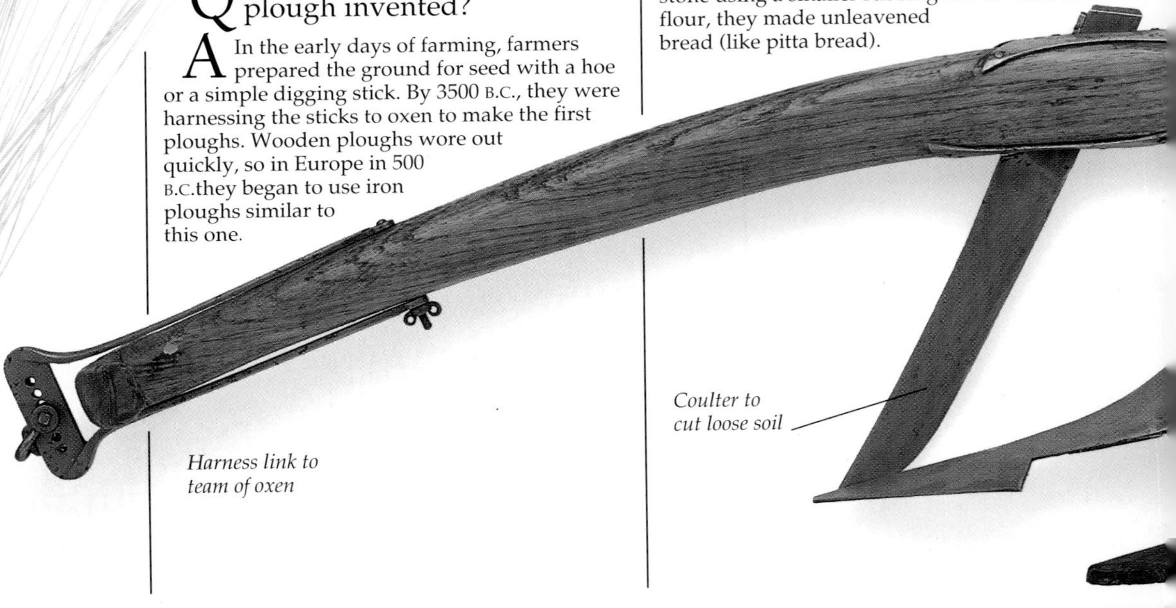

Harness link to team of oxen

Coulter to cut loose soil

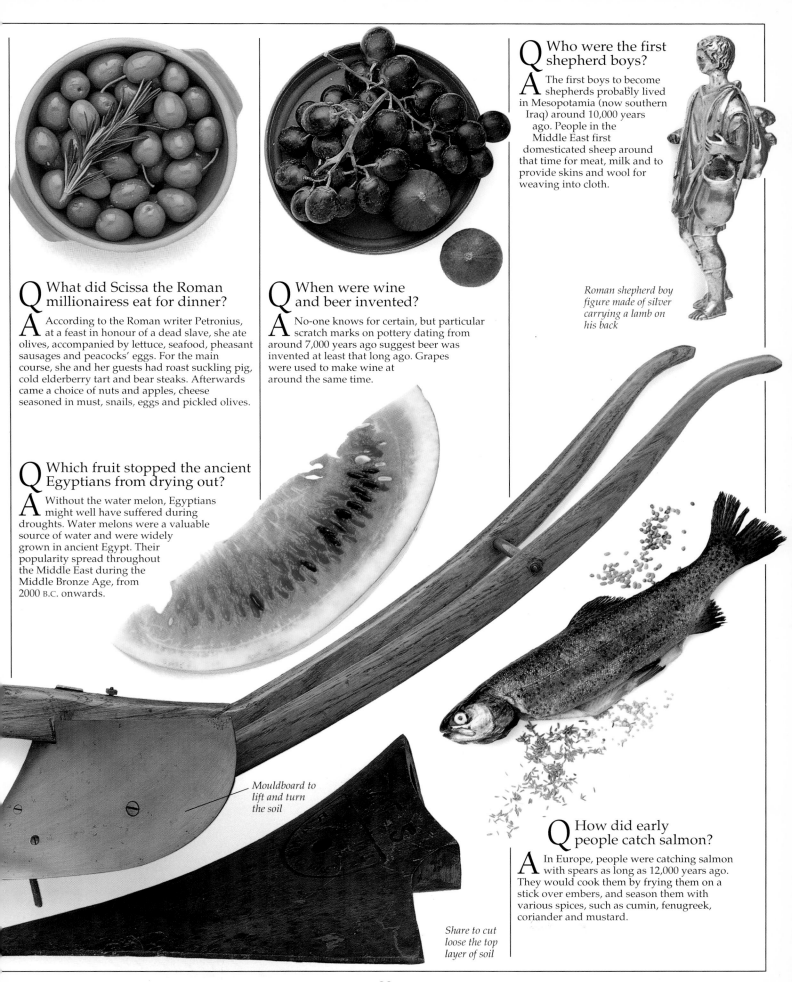

Q Who were the first shepherd boys?

A The first boys to become shepherds probably lived in Mesopotamia (now southern Iraq) around 10,000 years ago. People in the Middle East first domesticated sheep around that time for meat, milk and to provide skins and wool for weaving into cloth.

Roman shepherd boy figure made of silver carrying a lamb on his back

Q What did Scissa the Roman millionairess eat for dinner?

A According to the Roman writer Petronius, at a feast in honour of a dead slave, she ate olives, accompanied by lettuce, seafood, pheasant sausages and peacocks' eggs. For the main course, she and her guests had roast suckling pig, cold elderberry tart and bear steaks. Afterwards came a choice of nuts and apples, cheese seasoned in must, snails, eggs and pickled olives.

Q When were wine and beer invented?

A No-one knows for certain, but particular scratch marks on pottery dating from around 7,000 years ago suggest beer was invented at least that long ago. Grapes were used to make wine at around the same time.

Q Which fruit stopped the ancient Egyptians from drying out?

A Without the water melon, Egyptians might well have suffered during droughts. Water melons were a valuable source of water and were widely grown in ancient Egypt. Their popularity spread throughout the Middle East during the Middle Bronze Age, from 2000 B.C. onwards.

Mouldboard to lift and turn the soil

Q How did early people catch salmon?

A In Europe, people were catching salmon with spears as long as 12,000 years ago. They would cook them by frying them on a stick over embers, and season them with various spices, such as cumin, fenugreek, coriander and mustard.

Share to cut loose the top layer of soil

33

Who were the first merchants?

THE FIRST MERCHANTS probably appeared in the Middle East. Archaeologists excavating the remains of the ancient city of Ugarit in modern Iraq have found 10,000-year-old clay tokens that they may have used for buying and selling goods. By 4000 B.C., Sumerian merchants were travelling far and wide, trading food, cloth, pots and knives for timber, stone and metals.

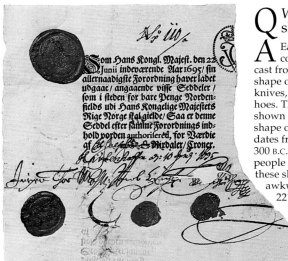

Q When were coins first used?

A The earliest known coins were made in the 7th century B.C. in Lydia in what is now Turkey. Lydian coins were simply lumps of electrum, a mixture of gold and silver, but each was weighed and stamped with pictures showing their value.

Ancient Greek silver coin, 6th century B.C.

Q Who had tool-shaped coins?

A Early Chinese coins were always cast from bronze in the shape of tools such as knives, sickles and hoes. The bronze coin shown here is in the shape of a hoe and dates from around 300 B.C. Eventually, people began to find these shapes awkward, and in 221 B.C. they were replaced by round coins with square holes.

Ancient Roman silver coin, 3rd century B.C.

Ancient Indian gold coin, 1st century A.D.

Australian aluminium-bronze 2-dollar coin, 1988

Q When did the first banknotes appear?

A In the 10th century, coins in China were so heavy and worth so little that people preferred to leave them with merchants and use the handwritten receipts the merchants gave them instead. In the 11th century, the government took over and began to issue printed receipts with fixed values – the first banknotes. The idea caught on in Europe in the 17th century, and Europe's first printed notes appeared in Sweden in 1661. The Norwegian note shown here dates from 1695.

Ottoman Turkish gold zeri-mahbub, 18th century

Ancient Roman gold bar, made from melted-down coins, 4th century A.D.

Q Who were the first great iron merchants?

A People probably discovered how to use iron to make tools and weapons around 8,000 years ago, but for a long time, the knowledge was restricted to a small area of the Middle East. The Hittite people who lived in what is now Turkey made a fortune selling iron in places such as Greece, and were probably the first great iron merchants. Eventually the Greeks learned to make iron themselves as this painting from a Greek urn shows.

Q What are coins made from?

A Many early coins were made from precious metals like gold and silver, and the value of the coin depended simply on the value of the metal they contained. Today, however, coins are usually made from cheap alloys such as cupro-nickel (copper and nickel) and the metal in the coin is worth much less than the value stamped on it at the mint.

Q Which stone went to Egypt?

A Merchants from what is now called Afghanistan used to trade the beautiful blue stone lapis lazuli with the ancient Egyptians. They brought it to trading centres like Byblos in Lebanon. The Egyptians prized this stone, because they believed the hair of their sun-god was made from lapis lazuli.

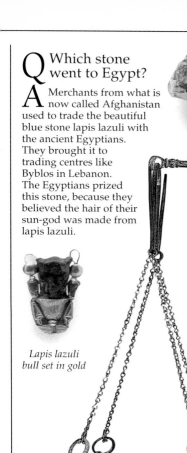

Lapis lazuli bull set in gold

Q How did Roman merchants weigh things?

This weight could be moved along the arm to multiply or divide the weight in the balance pan

A The might of the Roman empire ensured that merchants could trade safely everywhere from Britain to the Middle East, and Roman officials guaranteed a standard system of weights and measures. Merchants weighed everything from gold to vegetables on one of two types of scale: simple bronze balances and heavier steelyards with a hook for weighing large items such as bags of flour. The bronze weights were checked regularly by Roman officials to stop merchants cheating with false measures.

Q Which priests made money?

A When banknotes first appeared in Japan in the 17th century, it was not the government and banks that issued them but temples.

Japanese bookmark note of 1746

Cowrie shells from India

Q What goods were traded in stirrup jars?

A Stirrup jars were attractive pottery jars with handles shaped like a horserider's stirrups. They were made by the Myceneans of Greece between 1600 and 1100 B.C., and then sold in the Middle East, perhaps full of perfumed oils.

Q How did early Syrian merchants carry metal goods?

A Middle-Eastern merchants 5,000 years ago rode in covered wagons like those used in the Wild West in the late 19th century. This pottery model was found at Hamman in Syria.

Q Who or what was a corbita?

A A corbita was a small two-masted ship used by Roman merchants. In ships like these merchants ventured out into open water on long voyages across the Mediterranean rather than hug the coast as craft had done in earlier times.

Q How did early traders carry goods across deserts?

A Early traders in the Middle East relied on the one-humped Arabian camel when trekking across the desert. But around the 10th century B.C., two-humped Bactrian camels from Asia were introduced.

Q What did people use as money before coins and banknotes?

A Coins and banknotes are not the only form of money. For thousands of years, people have used everything from huge drilled stones to grains of rice as money. The use of cowrie shells as money dates back to China around 3,500 years ago. They have also been used in India, Thailand and Africa.

How was the world explored?

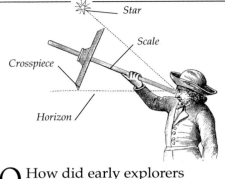

Star
Scale
Crosspiece
Horizon

SOME OF THE GREATEST JOURNEYS into the unknown were on foot like Marco Polo's travels in China in the 12th century, Livingstone's in Africa in the 1850s and Scott's in the Antarctic in the early 1900s. But it was sea voyages, above all, that steadily widened our knowledge of the world – starting 3,000 years ago with the Phoenicians and reaching a peak around 1500 with great seamen like Diaz, Columbus and Magellan.

Q Who discovered the secret of latitude?

A Arab explorers of the sixth and seventh centuries could find their approximate location at sea with a device called a quadrant. This was a quarter circle with a plumbline attached. They could work out latitude – how far north or south they were – by lining up one side with a star and reading off the position of the plumbline.

Q How did early explorers know where they were?

A On long sea voyages, the heavens provided early explorers with their only clue to where they were. In the 1500s, many used a cross-staff to work out the height of stars in the sky and hence the latitude of the ship.

Q Why did Scott take a chemistry set to the South Pole in 1910?

A Explorers often brought back immensely valuable scientific data. By carrying out simple chemical experiments, Robert Scott hoped to learn more about the minerals in the ancient rocks of Antarctica.

Q What was the seamen's curse – and who broke it?

A Early voyages of exploration were plagued by the disease scurvy – known as the seamen's curse. The first explorer to realize scurvy could be prevented by eating fresh fruit was James Cook (1728–1779), who broke the curse by taking citrus fruits and pickled cabbage on his voyage to the South Pacific in 1768.

Q Were all explorers' tales true?

A The temptation for explorers to elaborate tales of strange places and weird creatures must have been great, and in the 1800s all too many explorers were claiming to have discovered new species. By the time Mary Kingsley went to West Africa in the 1890s, naturalists wanted specimens to prove these species really did exist – which is why she carefully preserved this snoutfish found in the Ogowe River to bring it back to Britain.

Q Who first crossed the Atlantic?

A The question of who was the first to make it across the Atlantic arouses fierce passions, but we know the Vikings made the voyage 500 years before Columbus. In 1001, Leif Erikson set out from Greenland with a few longships like the one shown here to investigate rumours of a vast land to the southwest – and reached America. The Vikings called this land Vinland, and settled there for a century or so.

Q How did James Cook know where he was?

A Early seaborne explorers could find their direction with the aid of a magnetic compass – first used by the Chinese over 2,000 years ago. They could also find their latitude from the sun and stars. But they could only guess longitude – that is, how far east or west they were. On his second voyage Cook could not only find his latitude to within 0.01° with a sextant, but his longitude too, with a highly accurate clock called a chronometer, designed just a few years before by the ingenious Yorkshire clockmaker John Harrison.

Italian compass from 1719

The sextant used by Cook on his third voyage in 1776

Q What was the secret of Columbus's success?

A None of the great voyages of the 1400s – Diaz's around Africa (1487), Columbus's to the Americas (1492) and Da Gama's to India (1498) – could have been made without the caravel. Though small and light, these boats were fast enough for sailors to risk sailing far out across the ocean.

A chronometer used by Cook on his second voyage to the Pacific in 1772

Crow's-nest – used by the crew to look out for land, or hostile ships

Q Why did the Spanish go to America?

A In the hope, above all, of finding gold. Adventurers such as Francisco Pizarro and Hernán Cortés were lured to the New World by tales of the huge wealth of the Incas and Aztecs.

Q Why did Africa remain unexplored for so long?

A Mainly because it was dangerous. Not only were there tropical diseases that could kill a European in a day. There were also savage wild animals such as lions and crocodiles. And there were local people who sometimes resented invasion. The arrows below were fired into David Livingstone's boat as he explored the Zambezi River in the 1850s.

Large hold for carrying supplies

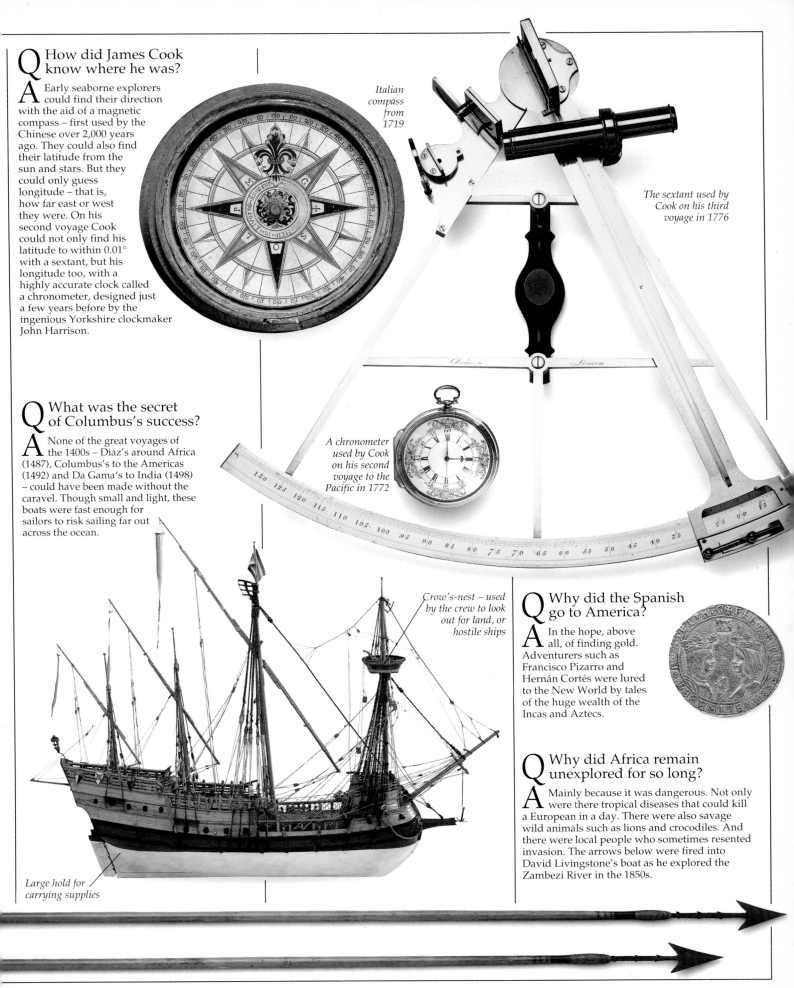

Why wear clothes?

HUMANS HAVE NO FUR or feathers to keep them warm and dry, nor do they have thick hides to protect them from thorns or scorching Sun – so they need to make their own body protection. The first clothes were probably animal skins that Ice-Age cave dwellers wrapped around themselves for warmth. Gradually, people learned to fit skins to their bodies with stitching, and about 10,000 years ago, the first woollen cloth was woven. But clothes do not only protect: they hide nakedness and may also show status.

Spring   *Pin*

Glass disc

Q How did Iron Age people fasten their clothes?

A In the days before safety pins and buttons, people used decorative brooches to fasten clothes. Buttons were not used until the 15th century. Many early brooches are very beautiful and testify to the skill of Iron Age craftsmen. The glass bow shown here is made up of glass discs and was probably worn by a person of high rank. It is from Italy and dates from between 800 and 700 B.C.

Q When did little boys wear dresses?

A From the late 18th to the late 19th century, many little boys – especially those from wealthier families – had to wear dresses up to the age of about six. They even had long curly hair. The idea that only girls can wear dresses and have their hair in ringlets is comparatively recent.

Boy's tunic dress from the early 19th century

Q When did men start wearing suits?

A During the 17th century, men started to wear long, full-skirted jackets with matching knee breeches, stockings, cravat and a waistcoat. This was the forerunner of the modern suit. Unlike the dull pinstripes of today, however, they were made of rich velvets and silk brocades, adorned with lacy frills and fancy buttons. Modern-style trousers did not come into being until the 1800s.

Deep, buttoned back cuff

Full-skirted jacket

Breeches

11th-century silver belt buckle

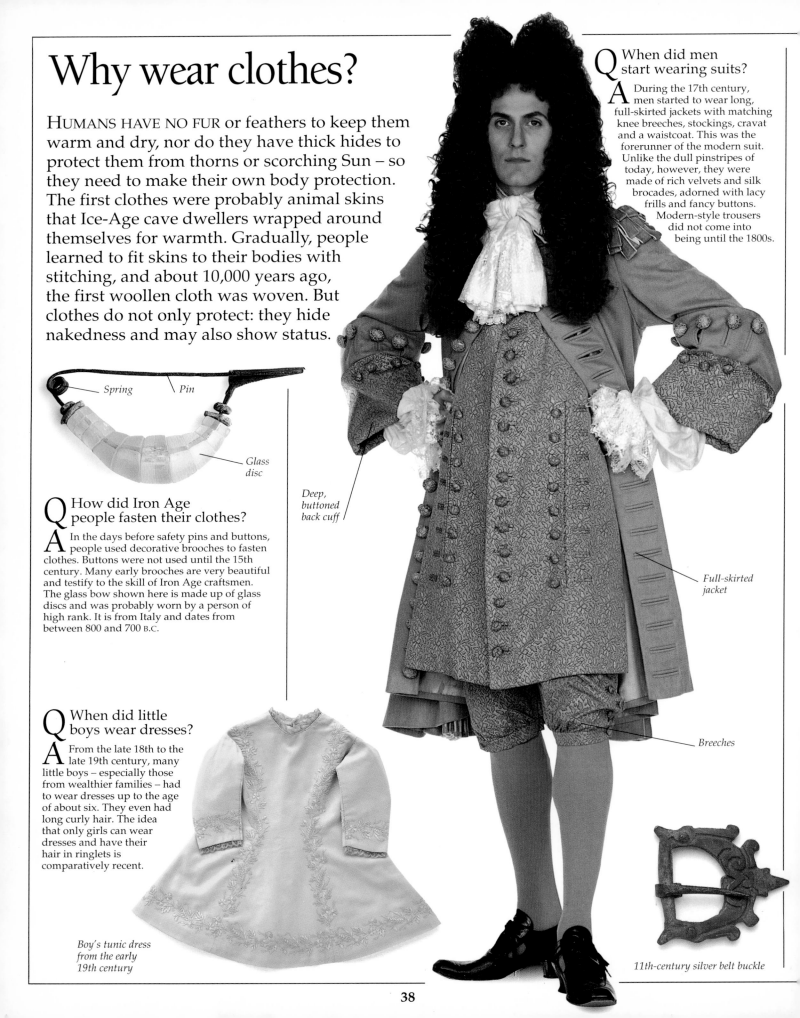

38

Q How did worms colour Greek life?

A Ancient Greek women loved to dye their chitons (dresses) in bright colours. One of their favourites was a rich crimson made from the skin of the tiny kermes worm which lives in the bark of holly and oak trees. During the day, the worms burrow deep inside the bark, but at night they come out on to the surface where girls with long nails picked them off.

Ancient Greek girl wearing a chiton

Q Who dressed in a cage?

A The cage crinoline was devised in 1856 to make skirts fashionably full. Until this time, women in the early 1800s had only achieved the desired fullness by wearing up to six heavy petticoats – one of which was stuffed with horsehair. Women could not wait to dress in cages.

Light steel wire hoops gave shape to the cage crinoline

Q When did children's fashion begin?

A Since the ancient civilizations of ancient Egypt, Rome and Greece, children have worn the same style of clothes as their parents. It was not until the late 18th century that children's clothes began to have a style of their own and their owners ceased to look like small adults. But during the 19th century children's styles were still very formal as this illustration shows. Only after World War II did children's clothes begin to have the casual style they have today.

Pair of Blackfoot moccasins

Q Who wore gold dolphin earrings?

A The ancient Romans often used dolphin motifs in art and for jewellery, like these two gold earrings. If a Roman saw a dolphin it was said to be a good omen and a promise of good weather. The Roman author Pliny told the story of a dolphin that carried a poor man's son to school each day. The story was probably inspired by ancient Greek coins that showed a picture of the son of the sea god Poseidon riding a dolphin.

Q When did vandals wear brooches?

A The Vandals were one of the German peoples that began to threaten the Roman Empire in the sixth century. The Romans thought all Germans were coarse and barbaric, but their spectacular jewellery proves otherwise. The beautiful brooch above was made by a German group called the Ostrogoths from silver, gold, green glass and red garnet in about A.D. 500.

Q When did people begin to wear high-heeled shoes?

A High heels were first worn in the late 16th century – by both women and men. Until this time, shoes had flat heels and took all kinds of bizarre shapes. Early in the 16th century, they were so wide that in England, Henry VIII decreed that no shoe should be wider than 15 cm (6 in). Back in the 14th century, the fashion was for long, pointed shoes. The toes could be 50 cm (20 in) long and were stuffed with moss to keep their shape. Such shoes were considered by the Church to be the work of the devil.

14th-century leather shoe

16th-century leather shoe

Q What could a Native American scout tell from a lost moccasin?

A Moccasins were the soft leather or buffalo rawhide shoes worn by Native Americans. Each tribe decorated shoes in a unique way with brightly coloured beads. So, if a mocassin was lost, a scout could tell which tribe it came from.

Q How did a 17th century gentleman do up his baldric?

A A baldric was a kind of sash worn over the shoulder to carry a sword or stick – and it was fastened with a buckle. Indeed, in the 17th century, buckles were used to fasten almost everything including baldrics, shoes, belts and breeches. Until about 1720, shoe buckles were small and plain. But then rich people began to wear huge diamond and silver buckles while poorer people made do with big steel, brass and quartz buckles.

Baldric buckle from c.1680

Diamond and silver buckle from c.1730

Silk-covered ladies' high-heeled shoe from c.1690

Who started athletics?

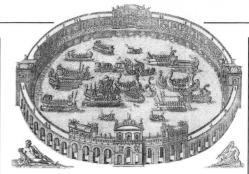

SPORTS have always played an important role in every society for players and spectators alike. Even prehistoric peoples would have taken pleasure from kicking a makeshift ball around or enjoyed the glory of winning a race against a rival. But the first regular sporting events were probably the athletic festivals held by the ancient Greeks. Here, young men would compete in the pentathlon, discus, long jump and track events.

Q What happened if the Roman *retiarius* lost his net?

A The Romans enjoyed much more bloody and sensational sports than the ancient Greeks. Tens of thousands of them would crowd into huge stadia to watch battles to the death between gladiators. One type of gladiator was the *retiarius*, or net man, who was unarmed apart from a net and a Neptune's trident. The aim was for the *retiarius* to catch his opponent in the net and stab him.But if he lost his net, he was usually doomed to die.

Gold glass picture of a retiarius *ready to do battle in the arena*

Q Why were there ships in the Colosseum?

A As Romans got bored with simple fighting games, they wanted to see more and more spectacular events. When it first opened, the arena of the Colosseum in Rome could be flooded with water so that "sea battles" could be fought between gladiators in small ships.

Competitors in the pentathlon

Q How did the marathon get its name?

A In 490 B.C. the Greeks won a heroic victory over the invading Persians on the plain of Marathon, northeast of Athens. At once, a young Greek runner called Pheidippides set off to Athens with the good news. Sadly, he died on arrival. However, over two thousand years later, in 1896, the first modern marathon was named in his honour and run over the distance from Marathon to Athens (26 miles 385 yd).

Q Where were the first Olympics held?

A The Olympic Games were the biggest of all the ancient Greek sporting festivals. They were staged every four years in Athens in honour of the god Zeus who lived on Mount Olympus on the Greek mainland. The ancient games died out in the fourth century A.D., but the spirit was revived when the first modern Olympics were held in Athens in 1896.

Q When did gloves become compulsory in boxing ?

A The bare knuckle fights popular in England in the 18th and 19th centuries were brutal. Boxing was reformed in 1867 with the introduction of the Queensberry Rules. The rules, which included three-minute rounds and wearing gloves, came into force in 1872.

Q How many games can you play with a ball?

A It would be almost impossible to name every ball game in the world, but almost every country has its favourites. The white ball shown here is used for American baseball; the red ball is a British cricket ball; the silver ball is used for the French game of boules; the black ball is a bowl which like the yellow golf ball is popular everywhere; and the small glass balls are marbles, which Roman children loved to play with.

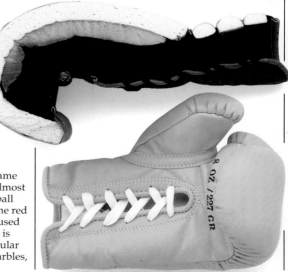

Lawn tennis racket from the 1880s

Fashionable fishtail-handle racket from the 1900s

Q **When were tennis rackets first used?**

A Tennis probably originated in the ancient French game of *jeu de paume*, played between two people who hit a ball to each other with the palms of their hands. After a while, players started to use sticks to hit the ball. Then in the 15th century, the first strung rackets were introduced. The basic shape of rackets has changed little since then, though materials are dfferent. Early rackets were made from wood, with gut strings. Modern rackets are moulded from light and strong new synthetic materials such as carbon fibre, fibreglass, boron and ceramic.

Q **How did softball and baseball begin?**

A People played games with a ball and long bat as long ago as the Middle Ages, but modern games of baseball and softball are probably based on the old English game of rounders, played with a smaller bat and introduced to North America by settlers during the 18th century.

Classic laminated wood racket from the 1950s

Q **How did badminton get its name ?**

A It is thought to be named after the home of the Duke of Beaufort at Badminton in Gloucestershire, England. Here in the 1870s the Duke's dinner guests played a parlour game called battledore and shuttlecock, adapted from a children's pastime. It involved hitting the shuttlecock to and fro over a net with a battledore (bat).

Metal racket from the 1970s enabling players to hit the ball faster

Moulded racket from the 1980s

Q **Why do runners wear spiked shoes?**

A Track athletes use spiked track shoes. These are tight fitting, lightweight, and the spikes give a good grip on the front of the sole where the foot touches the ground.

Counter of Quarte

Counter of Sixte

Counter of Septime

Counter of Seconde

Q **What is a Counter of Septime in fencing?**

A A Counter of Septime is one of various circular movements used to deflect the opponent's blade, beginning and ending with the sword angled downwards. As with many fencing terms, it originated in the 16th or 17th century, when the light court sword was introduced in France.

Who played a mammoth-bone flute?

HUMANS HAVE ENJOYED MUSIC for thousands of years. Around 20,000 years ago, Cro-Magnon people played mammoth-bone flutes, and archaeologists have discovered reindeer toe-bone whistles that date back 40,000 years. But the first music we know anything about was played by the Sumerians over 5,000 years ago in what is now Iraq. There are Sumerian signs that may be some of the first written music, pictures show lyres and harps, and a real 11-string harp was found in the royal tombs at Ur.

Q How could you play a goblet?

A Goblets are single-headed drums which are popular throughout the Arab world. Like the Egyptian darabuka shown here, they are usually made of pottery or wood and have a stretched skin beaten with both hands.

Q Who made the first panpipes?

A Pan was an ancient Greek god. When the nymph that he loved was turned into a reed, he cut the reed into a set of pipes, which he played to console himself. Today panpipes are popular in South America.

Q What kind of music does a Portuguese fish make?

A This fish-shaped *rajao* from Portugal is a kind of lute and would have been used for playing folk music in Madeira in the 19th century. Like all lutes it was plucked, rather like a guitar. The lute is one of the oldest instruments and the long lute, which has a long neck and short body, dates back at least 4,000 years. The European classical lute evolved from the *'ud*, an Arabian lute that reached Europe in the 13th century.

Q Which fiddle could fit in a pocket?

A In the 18th century, a dancing master would often use a kit, a pocket-sized violin, when he went to give lessons to young ladies at the great country houses. A kit was only 40 cm (16 in) long.

Q When is a fish like a recorder?

A This pottery fish doesn't look much like a recorder, but it makes music in just the same way. In both, a short duct (air channel) leads air from the mouth to blow-holes in the side. It is the vibration of the air in between that makes the sound.

Tuning peg

Lutes are plucked like the guitar and usually have a fretted fingerboard

Valve

Flared bell

Modern trumpet

Q Why is the trumpet a natural bandleader?

A The lead instrument in many bands and orchestras is often the trumpet because it can play loud, high notes and easily leads over softer and deeper instruments. The trumpet is a brass instrument often favoured by jazz musicians who make full use of the different moods that can be created. All the notes on a trumpet are achieved with just three valves.

Q Which dinosaur had a head for music?

A The hadrosaurs, which lived over 70 million years ago, had a long bony tube that extended into a crest behind the head. Dinosaur experts believe that some hadrosaurs, like this *Parasaurolophus*, may have been able to "talk" to each other by making sounds with these tubes – vibrating air inside them just as in a hunting horn.

Q What do Spanish dancers do with their castanets?

A Castanets are cup-shaped pieces of wood that Spanish flamenco dancers hold in the palms of their hands and clap together quickly to create an exciting, rhythmic click as they dance. Castanets are percussion instruments – which produce sounds when they are hit, or shaken.

Q Where does the harp originate?

A Harps are among the oldest of all instruments, and were invented independently in many places around the world. The Sumerians had them, and so too did the ancient Egyptians. There are wall paintings of Egyptian harps dating back over 4,000 years. The *tsaung* shown here is a modern instrument from Myanmar (Burma), but it is very similar to the harps of ancient Egypt.

Q Who invented the record player?

A In 1877, American inventor Thomas Alva Edison invented the first machine for recording sound, called a phonograph. It worked by scoring grooves on paraffin-soaked paper with a steel needle. A year later, he replaced the paper with tinfoil. But when the first recorded music went on sale in 1886, it was on wax cylinders. The gramophone, with flat discs, was invented in 1888 by E. Berliner.

Horn to amplify the sound

The music is recreated as the needle is vibrated by the little bumps in the record's groove

Early gramophone

Q What was Roman music like?

A The ancient Romans loved wild dances, especially at the riotous feasts of Cybele, when musicians would play frenzied music on a variety of instruments, such as pipes, lyres, horns and flutes. Although we know so much about the people and their instruments, we cannot be sure what Roman music itself was like but it may have been similar to modern Greek folk music.

Q Which instrument do you strap around your neck and squeeze?

A The accordion can be carried anywhere. It is supported by straps, leaving the musician's hands free to squeeze the bellows and press the keys and buttons. Pressing the keys and buttons allows air from the bellows to pass through sets of free metal reeds. Since they were invented in Berlin in the 1820s accordions have become popular with folk musicians around the world.

Who invented it?

SCIENCE AND TECHNOLOGY affect all of us in our daily lives. Every day we use machines and tools, travel on planes and trains, watch films and television, and take books and newspapers for granted. But how much do you know about the people who made and invented these machines and why? See if you can answer the questions here – then turn the pages and test your knowledge.

Why are racing cars faster than ordinary cars?

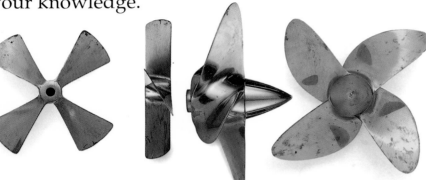

How did a tug-of-war make ships faster?

What was special about James Watt's engine?

Who revolutionized the revolver?

What was the first telephone message?

44

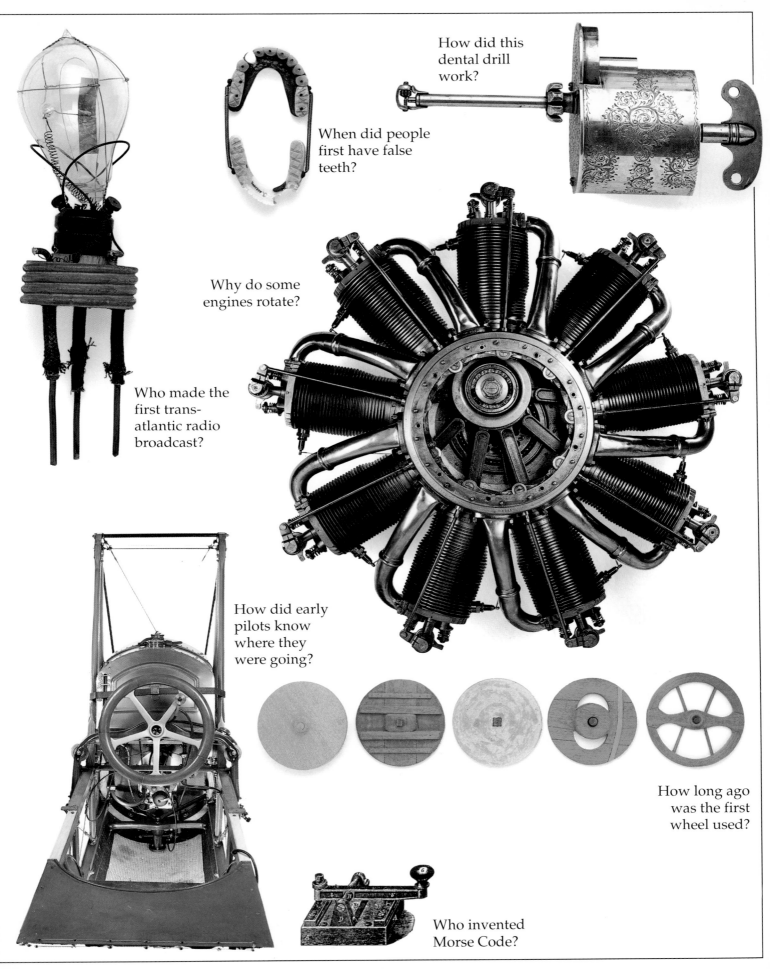

How did this dental drill work?

When did people first have false teeth?

Why do some engines rotate?

Who made the first trans-atlantic radio broadcast?

How did early pilots know where they were going?

How long ago was the first wheel used?

Who invented Morse Code?

45

Who made the first tools?

ALMOST AS SOON as they began to walk upright some 3.5 million years ago, our distant human-like ancestors began to use sharp stones for ripping meat and smashing animal bones. But the first real toolmakers were hominids like *Homo habilis* who emerged some 2 million years ago. Not for nothing does *Homo habilis* mean "handy man", for he was extremely handy with stone tools, chipping edges off stones not only to saw meat but to cut hides for clothing. By 400,000 years ago, people had learned to shape flint axes and spearheads.

Q How did early people make an axe from stone?

A Stone Age people became skilled at making axes, knives, and other cutting tools from stone. Using a stone, they could chip flakes off flints to get a sharp edge, as shown here. Firstly they trimmed the flint to a flat shape, and then knocked off a series of chips with another stone to give a rough edge. Finally the edge was sharpened and straightened by tapping with a bone hammer.

Shaping the core

Removing flakes

Finishing

Q How did the simple chisel revolutionize woodworking?

A Before the invention of chisels to shape wood into interlocking joints, wooden structures would have been crudely lashed. The first chisels were made in the late Stone Age by grinding and polishing stone. Later, in Egypt, some 3,000 years ago, fine bronze-bladed chisels were used for making furniture.

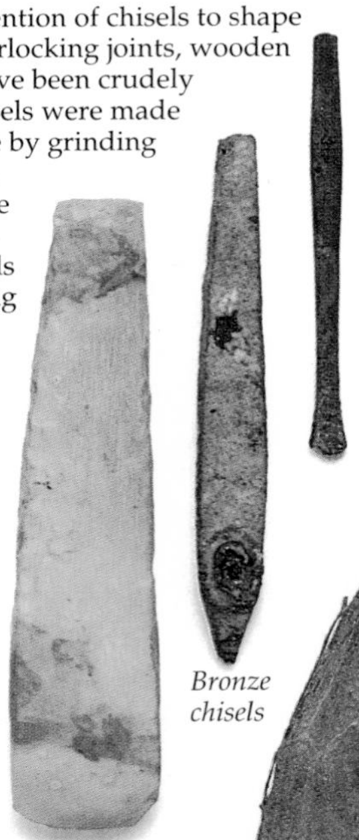

Bronze chisels

Stone chisel

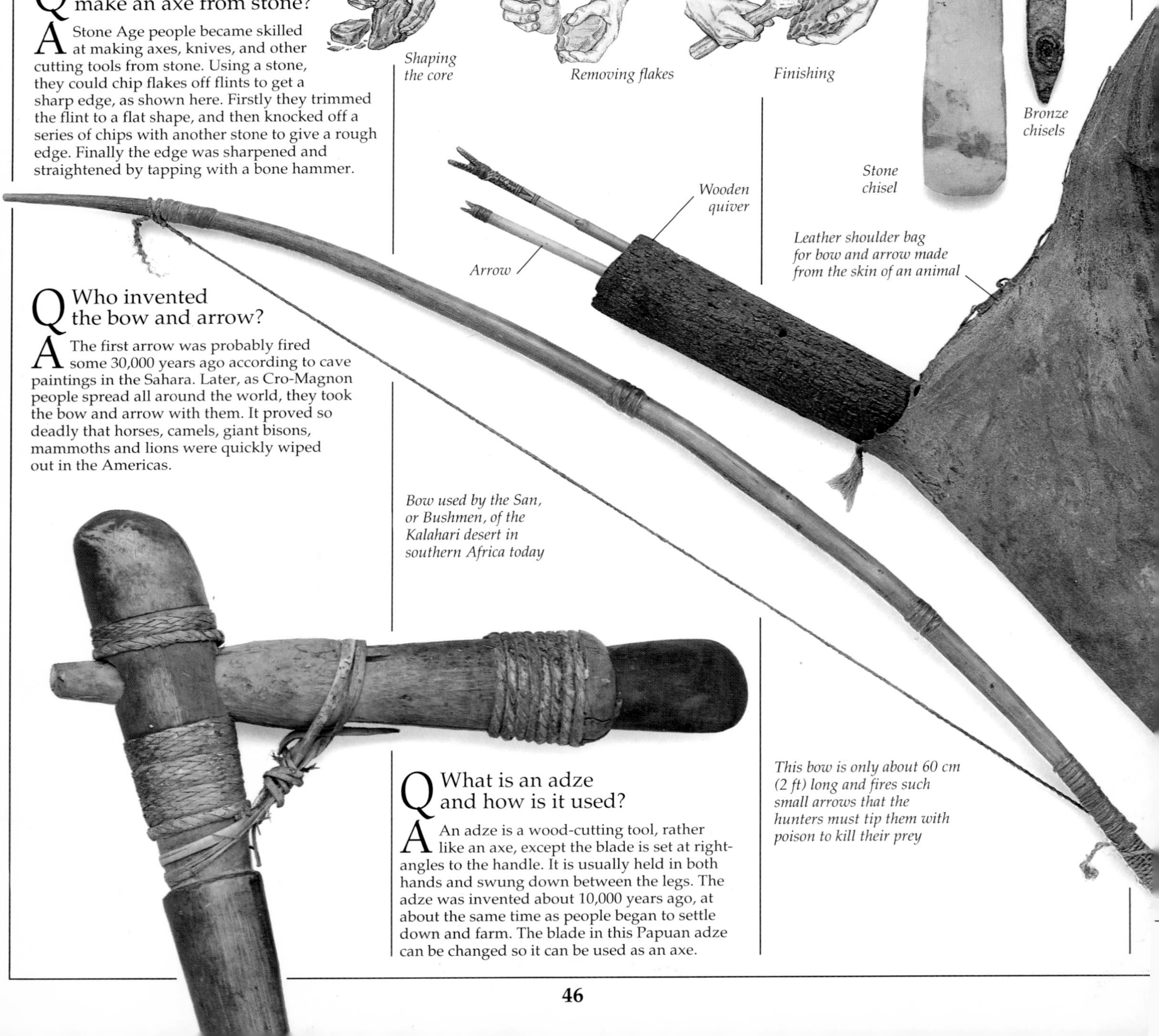

Wooden quiver

Arrow

Leather shoulder bag for bow and arrow made from the skin of an animal

Q Who invented the bow and arrow?

A The first arrow was probably fired some 30,000 years ago according to cave paintings in the Sahara. Later, as Cro-Magnon people spread all around the world, they took the bow and arrow with them. It proved so deadly that horses, camels, giant bisons, mammoths and lions were quickly wiped out in the Americas.

Bow used by the San, or Bushmen, of the Kalahari desert in southern Africa today

Q What is an adze and how is it used?

A An adze is a wood-cutting tool, rather like an axe, except the blade is set at right-angles to the handle. It is usually held in both hands and swung down between the legs. The adze was invented about 10,000 years ago, at about the same time as people began to settle down and farm. The blade in this Papuan adze can be changed so it can be used as an axe.

This bow is only about 60 cm (2 ft) long and fires such small arrows that the hunters must tip them with poison to kill their prey

Q What is unusual about these knives?

A They were made by Inuit (Eskimos) out of scraps of steel found in ships abandoned in the Arctic by Sir John Franklin on his fatal last trip in 1845. They sharpened the steel and attached the blades to handles made of bone.

The natural colouring in the safflower, or dyers' thistle, was used 4,000 years ago to dye cloth red and yellow

Early spindle

Straps made from animal's legs

Inuit knives made from steel and bone

Main handle

Winch

Main wheel

Q How were the first woollen clothes made?

A The first woollen clothes were probably made about 10,000 years ago by people in the Middle East, which is where sheep were first domesticated. The raw wool was plucked off the back of the sheep when it was moulting, spun into a single thread using a spindle, and then woven into cloth. The first woollen cloth was not coloured, but by 3000 B.C., people had learned how to dye it bright colours using natural dyes.

Q How did people start fires before matches were invented?

A By turning the point of a kind of wooden drill very fast on a block of wood, early people generated enough friction and heat to start a fire in dry grass. Some people twisted the drill by hand; others used a bow in the way shown below. The leather thong made it easier to twist the drill quickly.

Model of a bow drill

Using a bow drill

Wooden hearth showing holes where the drill has been used

Pinion

Chuck

Q How do gearwheels work?

A This brace drill, used for working in confined spaces, incorporates some of the most basic engineering principles. The wheels are adapted as gears and pinions and the drill bit is in the form of a screw to give it better forward motion. The use of gears means that the turning force of the handle is increased and transmitted down to the bit.

47

What was the first weapon?

THE FIRST WEAPONS were the stones prehistoric people used for hunting over 300,000 years ago. These were revolutionized by adding a handle or haft to make spears and axes. The invention of the bow some 30,000 years ago was another major step, and the coming of metals in the Bronze Age enabled swords to be made. Swords gave way to firearms in the 1700s.

Q What did a pistol owner carry in his flask?

A Gunpowder. Until self-contained cartridges were introduced in the mid-19th century, pistols had to be loaded through the muzzle. First, gunpowder was poured from the flask into the muzzle of the gun. Then the lead bullet was wrapped in a cloth or leather patch and rammed into the muzzle with a metal or wooden ramrod.

Colt "Peacemaker" single-action Army revolver

Colt .41 calibre pocket pistol

Q Who revolutionized the revolver?

A Samuel Colt (1814–1862) was only 21 when he patented his new "revolver". During his lifetime, Colt manufactured some of the best revolvers in the world including the Colt 45 and the popular Colt Peacemaker which is still made today. He even made tiny pistols like the .41 calibre Colt – which was ideal for gamblers to slip out of their pocket in a tricky situation.

Q How were lead bullets made?

A Flintlock pistols were popular in the 18th century, replacing swords for duels between gentlemen. The lead ball or bullet was made at home, using a special bullet-shaped mould that came with the pistol. Lead was melted over a fire and poured into the mould. After a few seconds the mould was opened like a pair of scissors and the ball shaken out. Any excess lead was trimmed off with shears.

Q What is a backsword?

A A backsword is a kind of military sword used by European cavalry in the 17th century for both cutting and thrusting at an opponent in battle. Like all swords of the the time, it was much lighter and easier to handle than the massive swords of the Middle Ages. Fighting with swords like these was a highly skilled art.

Q Why might an archer value a pavise?

A A pavise was a large shield that medieval archers and crossbowmen would shelter behind while firing their weapons. Used between the 14th and the 16th centuries, the pavise was as big as a man and made of wood covered with canvas. Since the archer needed both hands for firing his bow, the pavise was usually supported by another soldier. The pavise shown here dates from the mid-15th century and was commonly used in siege warfare.

48

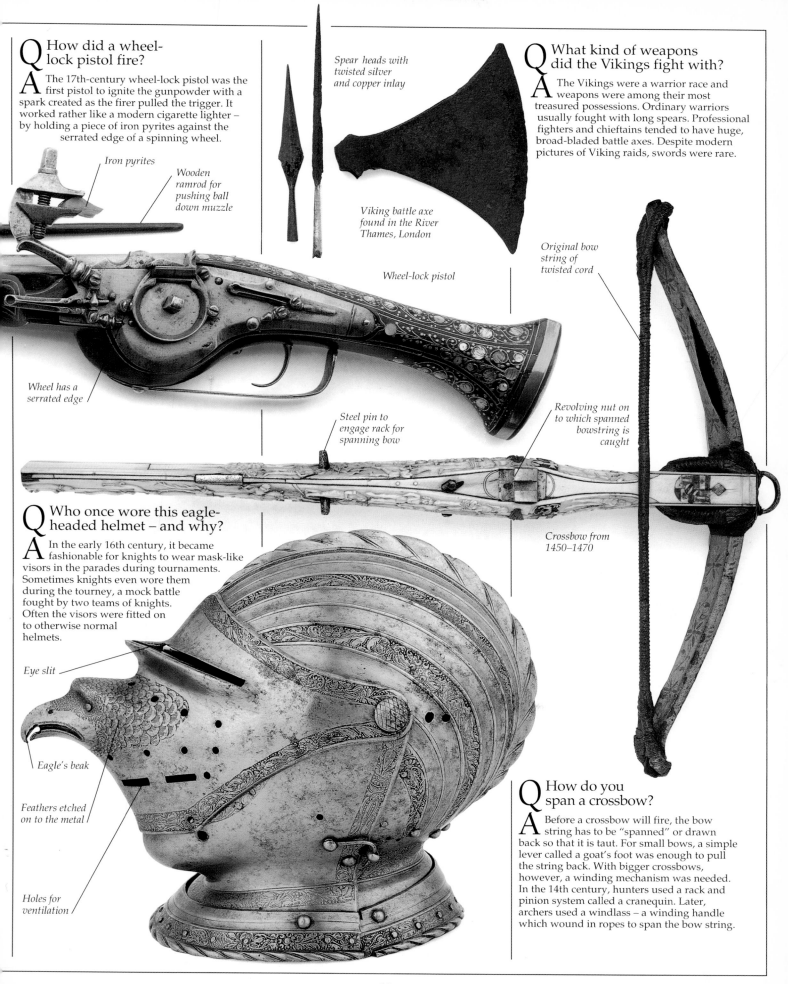

Q How did a wheel-lock pistol fire?

A The 17th-century wheel-lock pistol was the first pistol to ignite the gunpowder with a spark created as the firer pulled the trigger. It worked rather like a modern cigarette lighter – by holding a piece of iron pyrites against the serrated edge of a spinning wheel.

Iron pyrites

Wooden ramrod for pushing ball down muzzle

Wheel has a serrated edge

Spear heads with twisted silver and copper inlay

Viking battle axe found in the River Thames, London

Wheel-lock pistol

Q What kind of weapons did the Vikings fight with?

A The Vikings were a warrior race and weapons were among their most treasured possessions. Ordinary warriors usually fought with long spears. Professional fighters and chieftains tended to have huge, broad-bladed battle axes. Despite modern pictures of Viking raids, swords were rare.

Original bow string of twisted cord

Steel pin to engage rack for spanning bow

Revolving nut on to which spanned bowstring is caught

Crossbow from 1450–1470

Q Who once wore this eagle-headed helmet – and why?

A In the early 16th century, it became fashionable for knights to wear mask-like visors in the parades during tournaments. Sometimes knights even wore them during the tourney, a mock battle fought by two teams of knights. Often the visors were fitted on to otherwise normal helmets.

Eye slit

Eagle's beak

Feathers etched on to the metal

Holes for ventilation

Q How do you span a crossbow?

A Before a crossbow will fire, the bow string has to be "spanned" or drawn back so that it is taut. For small bows, a simple lever called a goat's foot was enough to pull the string back. With bigger crossbows, however, a winding mechanism was needed. In the 14th century, hunters used a rack and pinion system called a cranequin. Later, archers used a windlass – a winding handle which wound in ropes to span the bow string.

49

Who was the first true doctor?

THERE HAVE BEEN HEALERS and medicine men since prehistoric times. But the father of modern medicine was the Greek physician Hippocrates (circa 460–380 B.C.), who based his treatments on careful study of the body. He believed that diet and hygiene were the first essentials of good health. The Hippocratic Oath that many doctors take when they begin to practise is named after him.

The Harrington "Eardo" clockwork dental drill, dating from about 1863

Breathing sack placed over the patient's mouth

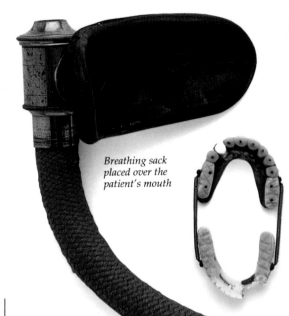

Q When did people first have false teeth?

A The first full set of false teeth like those today was made in France in the 1780s. The set shown here, though, dates from about 1860 – about the same time as dentists started to drill teeth to try to get rid of decay. Crude dentures were made by the Etruscans of Italy about 2,700 years ago.

Ancient Egyptian amulets

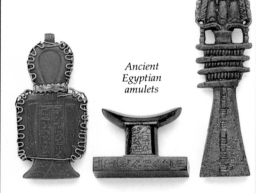

Q Why might a Roman make a model ear?

A Ancient Romans and Greeks believed injuries and ailments could be cured more quickly if they donated a votive model of the afflicted part to the gods. So when Romans visited the temple to ask for a cure for earache, they would leave behind a model ear. They might also leave a votive offering in gratitude once the ear was better.

Greek model leg offered in thanks for a cure to the god Asclepius

Q Why did the ancient Egyptians wear charm bracelets?

A The ancient Egyptians wore bracelets with special magical amulets dangling from them. Spells were often cast on these amulets and the Egyptians believed they would ward off injury.

The drink mescal made from Agave tequilana

Mescal cactus

Coca leaves

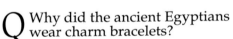

Q Which South American plants contain addictive drugs?

A Many do, but the best known are the coca plant and the Mexican mescal cactus. The natives of South America discovered long ago that chewing the leaves of the coca plant dulled pain and prevented tiredness. Today, people derive the stimulating and dangerous drug cocaine from coca leaves. Cocaine is highly addictive and there is a huge illegal trade in it from Colombia. The mescal cactus yields a drug called mescaline, which causes hallucinations. It is often used in religious rituals by native Mexican tribes. Confusingly, the Mexican drink mescal comes not from the mescal cactus but from another plant, *Agave tequilana*.

50

Breathing tube

Castor-oil plant

Microscope slide
showing prehistoric
micro-organism

Rhabdomeson
Gracile. Phil.
horizontal and
vertical sections.

(60524)

Capelrig nr.
East Kilbride
Lanarkshire.
Carb. Lime Series
from
Dr Young & J. Young.

Anaesthetic
gas vaporizes
from ether-
soaked
sponges

Eyepiece lens

Foxglove

19th-century
microscope
similar to that
used by
Pasteur

Magnifying
lens

R 1978/1936

A625399

Q What is castor oil?

A Oil made from the beans of the castor-oil plant, used to purify the system since the days of ancient Egypt. The beans also contain the powerful poison ricin.

Q Why are foxgloves good for the heart?

A They contain the essence of the drug digitalis, used to stimulate the heart. Overdoses of digitalis, though, can cause palpitations and dizziness.

Q Why would anyone want to eat a rhinoceros's horn?

A Because rhino horn can be ground into a powder that is supposed to be an aphrodisiac – that is, a substance that excites sexual desire.

Q Who conducted the first operation under anaesthetic?

A In 1844, an American dentist Horace Wells (1815–1848) put himself to sleep with nitrous oxide (laughing gas) while having a tooth extracted. Two years later, his pupil William Morton invented an anaesthetic machine similar to the one shown here.

Q Who realized disease was carried by microscopic germs?

A Bacteria were seen for the first time in the 17th century when a Dutch scientist, Anton van Leeuwenhoek (1632–1723), looked down his microscope at scrapings of the white film on his teeth. But the idea that bacteria were germs which caused disease was proposed by the French chemist Louis Pasteur (1822–1895) in the late 1800s.

Q How did the Romans operate?

A Roman surgeons performed operations in much the same way that surgeons do today, and used many of the same instruments. Shown here are hooks for holding sinews and blood vessels out of the way during the operation. But there were no anaesthetics, nor any idea of sterilization, so operations were agonizing and dangerous.

51

How fast can a message be sent?

FOR THOUSANDS OF YEARS THE ONLY WAY TO get a complicated message over any distance was to carry it physically – which made communication very slow. Even in 1649 it took over a week for people in northern England to learn that Charles I had been executed. Today, modern electronics enable us to send words, pictures and sounds almost instantaneously across the world via telephones, radio, television and other media.

Q Who invented printing?

A The Chinese made printed books like this one as long ago as the sixth century A.D. They used characters engraved on a block of wood, clay or ivory, which was inked and pressed against the paper. By the 11th century, the Chinese were using movable type – single characters on small individual blocks that could be set in any order and used again and again.

Casts of early Turkish type

Diode valve

Q Who was the first person to appear on television?

A When a Scottish inventor, John Logie Baird, was experimenting with television he paid a 15-year-old office boy called Bill Taynton half-a-crown (12.5p) to appear on the screen in October 1925. Baird gave the world's first public demonstration of television the following January and became famous overnight. Ten years later, the BBC began to broadcast television pictures from its studio at Alexandra Palace in London, shown above.

Q Who printed the Bible first?

A In about 1438 a German goldsmith, Johannes Gutenberg, invented "typecasting" – a way of making type of individual letters from molten metal. These letters could then be set by hand on the page ready for printing. He completed the first printed Bible in 1455.

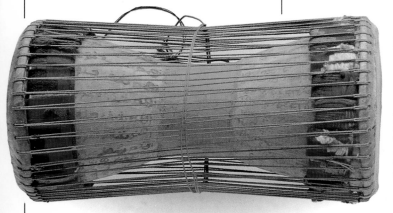

Q Can a drum talk?

A Yes. Nigerians use this *kalengo* to "talk" by pressing the cords to raise or lower the note produced as they beat the drum. The drum makes the sound of a tonal, African language and can communicate very complex messages.

Q Who made the first transatlantic radio broadcast?

A In 1901, an Italian inventor, Guglielmo Marconi (1874–1937), sent the first radio signal across the Atlantic from Poldhu in Cornwall to St. John's in Newfoundland, Canada. These early radio signals were very faint and were picked up by certain crystals that allowed current to pass only in one direction. In 1904, however, an English electrical engineer John Ambrose Fleming invented the diode or tube which picked up the signals much better. Two years later, in 1906, an American inventor Lee De Forest added an extra element to make a triode, which enabled the signal to be amplified.

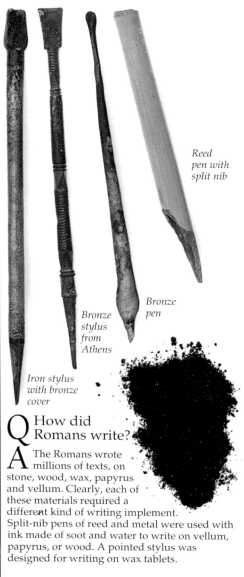

Reed pen with split nib

Bronze pen

Bronze stylus from Athens

Iron stylus with bronze cover

Q What was the first telephone message?

A In 1875, a Scots inventor, Alexander Graham Bell, constructed the first experimental telephone. Then on 10 March 1876, he transmitted the first telephone message to a colleague in a room upstairs: "Mr Watson, come here. I want to see you." Within a few years, people were calling each other on telephones like the wall-mounted phone shown here, designed by Thomas Edison in 1879.

Earpiece

Mouthpiece

The user had to wind the handle while listening

Q How did Romans write?

A The Romans wrote millions of texts, on stone, wood, wax, papyrus and vellum. Clearly, each of these materials required a different kind of writing implement. Split-nib pens of reed and metal were used with ink made of soot and water to write on vellum, papyrus, or wood. A pointed stylus was designed for writing on wax tablets.

Q How did bees help Roman writers?

A Roman writers often wrote everyday letters on wax. Beeswax was melted and poured into shallow cavities in wooden tablets. When it hardened, people could scratch their message with a sharp stylus.

Q How do gypsy moths communicate?

A Female gypsy moths produce a very faint scent (a pheromone), which can attract males from as far as 11 km (7 miles) away.

Q Who invented Morse code?

A An American, Samuel Morse, patented Morse code in 1838. Every letter of the alphabet was represented by a series of dots and dashes. Morse's code was adopted by the first electric telegraphs when they came into operation in 1843. The telegraph allowed signals to be sent along a wire by switching on and off an electric current. By tapping on an electric switch, operators could send messages over long distances.

Q What is semaphore?

A Semaphore is a method of signalling with flags in different positions. It was invented in the 18th century to help ships keep in touch at sea, but is very rarely used nowadays.

"Ready" position

The letter E

The letter X

Who invented movies?

THE FIRST MOVIES were made by a French inventor, Louis Le Prince, as long ago as 1888. He shot pictures of traffic moving on a bridge in Leeds in northern England, using a special camera to take scores of pictures in a few minutes on light-sensitive rolls of paper. The first film lasting much more than a minute, though, was made the following year by the American inventor, Thomas Edison, and his British assistant, William Dickson. In their short film, according to contemporary newspaper reports, a man "bowed and smiled, and took off his hat with the most perfect naturalness and grace".

Heavy magazines hold three strips of film separately

Viewfinder window shows the camera operator what is being filmed

Matt-box (lens hood) keeps stray light out of the lens

Light-tight door

Q What was the first film in colour?

A *Becky Sharp*, a historical drama based on Thackeray's *Vanity Fair*, was the first real colour film, made in 1935 with the Technicolor three-strip process. The Technicolor process worked by making three separate black-and-white films for the red, blue and green parts of the scenes using a special camera with a beam-splitting prism.

Q Who made the first rolls of film?

A Early photographs were all taken on cumbersome glass and metal plates in big, heavy cameras. Paper roll films were first used in 1887 by a French scientist, Étienne Marey. In 1888, American George Eastman launched a small lightweight camera called the Kodak, which used paper films instead of plates. A year later, Kodak introduced rolls of film on celluloid.

Wet-plate collodion chemicals

Q What did early photographers put on a wet plate?

A Early photographs. In 1851 Frederick Scott Archer invented a way of taking photographs using a glass photographic plate that was more light-sensitive than its predecessors. Called the wet-plate collodion process, it consisted of a glass plate, which was coated with silver salts and a sticky material called collodion. The plate was put in the camera and exposed while it was still wet. It was a messy process but gave excellent results. After exposure the image was developed and fixed using chemicals dispensed from small bottles.

Tripod to keep the camera steady during filming

Wheels made the camera easy to move

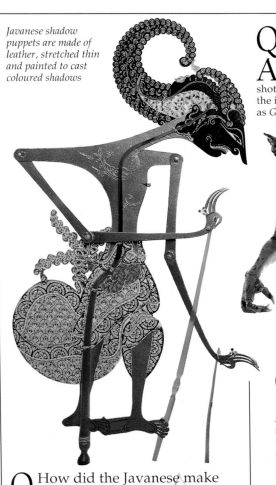

Javanese shadow puppets are made of leather, stretched thin and painted to cast coloured shadows

Q How do you make a gremlin?

A Monsters in films like *King Kong* were rubber models which were moved and shot painstakingly frame by frame to create the illusion of movement. Today, films such as *Gremlins* rely on animatronics which creates working models that move and can be shot just like any live actor. Under remarkably realistic latex skins, electronic motors operate steel joints and muscles to create the most life-like movements. Computerization – especially virtual reality techniques – makes even very complex sequences possible.

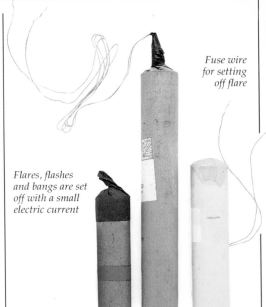

Fuse wire for setting off flare

Flares, flashes and bangs are set off with a small electric current

Q Who set the *Towering Inferno* ablaze?

A Films like *Towering Inferno* rely on realistic fire and explosion sequences. Because they are potentially very dangerous, these sequences are always handled by experts called pyrotechnicists who ensure every fire and explosion is very carefully planned and controlled. For a controllable blaze, sets are built with flaming forks. These are gas jets that burn with real flames that can be extinguished when the director shouts "cut". Explosions are set off from a safe distance with an electric current and some may be big enough to create huge balls of fire.

Cap indicates the colour of the smoke in the cylinder

Q How did the Javanese make movies over 400 years ago?

A With shadow puppets – puppets designed to cast a shadow that can be moved at will with sticks that swivel jointed limbs. Javanese shadow puppets were used to tell traditional tales with a narrator and orchestra. The idea spread to Europe in the 17th century, and in 1893 the Chicago World Fair featured a shadow show.

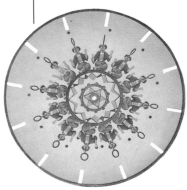

As the disc turns the horse jumps through the hoop

Q What is a Phenakistoscope?

A A device for creating the illusion of movement by using images on a rapidly spinning disc. It was invented in 1833 by a Belgian physicist, Joseph Plateau (1801–1883). All the pictures on the disc were slightly different, so that as the disc spun, they all blurred together into one apparently moving image.

Q What was the first successful photographic process?

A The daguerreotype invented by Louis Jacques Daguerre (1789–1851) in 1839. This process used a plain copper plate coated with a silver compound made sensitive to light by letting iodine vapour pass over it. Once the photograph was taken, the plate was developed by passing mercury vapour over it, and the image fixed permanently with a salt solution. Mercury vapour is highly toxic, so the process could be dangerous.

What is natural energy?

NEARLY ALL THE WORLD'S NATURAL ENERGY, from muscle power to running water, comes originally from the Sun. The Sun delivers over 99 per cent of the energy that reaches the Earth's surface; the tiny remaining fraction is heat from the Earth's hot interior and tidal power created by the gravitational pull of the Sun and Moon on the water in the oceans. The Sun's energy stirs up the atmosphere to create winds and rain and gives life to plants which in turn provide energy to the animals that feed on them.

Studding sails

Tail post

Q How did a post mill change with the wind?

A Post mills had a large post running right up the middle, on which the whole mill could swivel to face the sails into the wind. In early post mills, the miller turned the mill's sails into the wind manually by pushing on a long tail post extending out behind the mill. Later mills had a small wind wheel called a fantail that turned the mill automatically.

Q How would you power a curragh?

A The traditional Irish curragh relies on the muscles of two people to propel it through the wild Atlantic surf on the west coast of Ireland. The curragh, which is still used for fishing, is made from cattle hides or canvas stretched over a light willow frame.

Q What are studding sails?

A Studding sails (pronounced stuns'ls) were extra sails hung from short yards and booms extending beyond the normal sails. From early in the 18th century, they were carried by all sailing ships, such as this brig from the 1850s, to keep the ship moving well even in light breezes.

Q Why do we need sugar to move?

A The sugar we buy is almost pure glucose, the fuel that powers all muscles – which is why athletes often eat sweet glucose tablets to give them extra energy. But the body does not need to rely on purified sugar for muscle power. In a complex chemical process, it can create its own glucose from any food that contains starches.

Q How does sea power make the beach sandy?

A Rocks falling from cliffs are broken down into smaller and smaller pieces as they are hurled together by the power of the waves. Eventually they are smashed into fine sand. Water naturally sorts the grains into different sizes and deposits each in a different place. Generally the biggest pebbles are furthest up the beach where they are flung by storm waves.

Q Where do the world's fastest horses come from?

A The fastest horses are thoroughbred racehorses, which descend from Arabian and Barb breeds. Arab horses probably orginated not in Arabia as their name suggests but in Egypt, where they were used over 3,500 years ago. The Barb comes from Morocco in northern Africa.

56

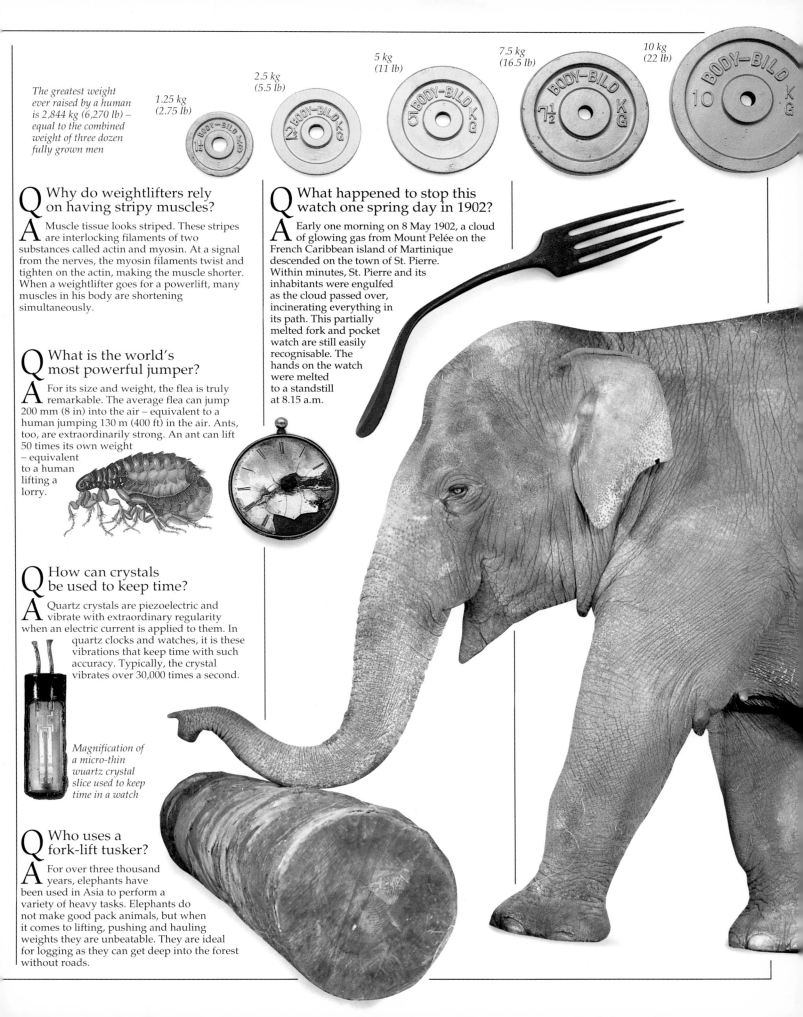

The greatest weight ever raised by a human is 2,844 kg (6,270 lb) – equal to the combined weight of three dozen fully grown men

1.25 kg (2.75 lb)

2.5 kg (5.5 lb)

5 kg (11 lb)

7.5 kg (16.5 lb)

10 kg (22 lb)

Q Why do weightlifters rely on having stripy muscles?

A Muscle tissue looks striped. These stripes are interlocking filaments of two substances called actin and myosin. At a signal from the nerves, the myosin filaments twist and tighten on the actin, making the muscle shorter. When a weightlifter goes for a powerlift, many muscles in his body are shortening simultaneously.

Q What is the world's most powerful jumper?

A For its size and weight, the flea is truly remarkable. The average flea can jump 200 mm (8 in) into the air – equivalent to a human jumping 130 m (400 ft) in the air. Ants, too, are extraordinarily strong. An ant can lift 50 times its own weight – equivalent to a human lifting a lorry.

Q How can crystals be used to keep time?

A Quartz crystals are piezoelectric and vibrate with extraordinary regularity when an electric current is applied to them. In quartz clocks and watches, it is these vibrations that keep time with such accuracy. Typically, the crystal vibrates over 30,000 times a second.

Magnification of a micro-thin wuartz crystal slice used to keep time in a watch

Q Who uses a fork-lift tusker?

A For over three thousand years, elephants have been used in Asia to perform a variety of heavy tasks. Elephants do not make good pack animals, but when it comes to lifting, pushing and hauling weights they are unbeatable. They are ideal for logging as they can get deep into the forest without roads.

Q What happened to stop this watch one spring day in 1902?

A Early one morning on 8 May 1902, a cloud of glowing gas from Mount Pelée on the French Caribbean island of Martinique descended on the town of St. Pierre. Within minutes, St. Pierre and its inhabitants were engulfed as the cloud passed over, incinerating everything in its path. This partially melted fork and pocket watch are still easily recognisable. The hands on the watch were melted to a standstill at 8.15 a.m.

How old is steam power?

STEAM POWER dates back to the first century A.D. when the Greek scientist Hero of Alexandria described the "aeolipile" – a simple device that used steam power to turn a wheel. But it was 1,500 years before people developed a way of using steam to drive machinery. In 1698, Thomas Savery (c. 1650–1715) patented the first steam-engine for pumping water from mines and it was only a matter of time before steam power was used to move trains and ships. But people continued to look for more efficient sources of power leading to the development of electric, petrol and diesel engines.

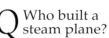

Q Who made the first battery?

A In 1800, Alessandro Volta (1745–1827) published details of his first chemical battery. It consisted of layers of zinc and silver or copper sandwiched between blotting paper pads soaked in sulphuric acid. Modern batteries, like the ones used in torches and radios, are known as "dry" cell batteries. These follow the same basic design of the first batteries, but use modern materials.

Q How did the first steam pump work?

A Thomas Savery's steam pump was used in mines in 1698. Steam from a boiler passed into a pair of vessels. The steam was condensed back into water, sucking water up from the mine below. Using stop cocks and valves, steam pressure was then directed to push the water up a vertical outlet pipe.

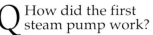

Q Why do some engines revolve?

A One of the main problems of early aero-engines was that they often overheated. But in 1908, the French Seguin brothers brought out the rotary engine in which the cylinders rotated around the central crankshaft. This created a constant flow of air over them and so kept them cool.

Q Who built a steam plane?

A The first aero engine was a steam engine, built by two Englishmen, William Henson and John Stringfellow, in 1845 to power their "Aerial Steam Carriage". This model steam plane was the first ever practical design for a powered aircraft. But steam engines proved either too weak or too heavy and it was not until the invention of the petrol engine that powered flight became possible.

Cylinder and engine pulley from Henson and Stringfellow's model engine

Q How did a frog teach scientists how to store electricity?

A In about 1790, an Italian professor, Luigi Galvani (1737–1798), noted that a dead frog twitched when touched with two different metals at the same time. Galvani put this phenomenon down to "animal electricity". Soon after, Volta proved the twitching was caused as the metals reacted with the moisture in the frog's body and produced electricity. This discovery led him to devise the first battery.

Q Why do some cars have spark plugs?

A All vehicles that run on petrol have spark plugs which deliver an electric spark to each of the engine's cylinders at the right moment to ignite the fuel. When the fuel burns it expands and pushes the piston down, giving the engine its power. In diesel engines there is no need for a spark, as the pressure created by the piston when it rises is enough to light the fuel.

Q What was special about James Watt's engine?

A In 1769, James Watt made the first really efficient steam engine. Unlike earlier engines, the steam condensed outside rather than inside the cylinder which caused it to cool down and reduce the heat.

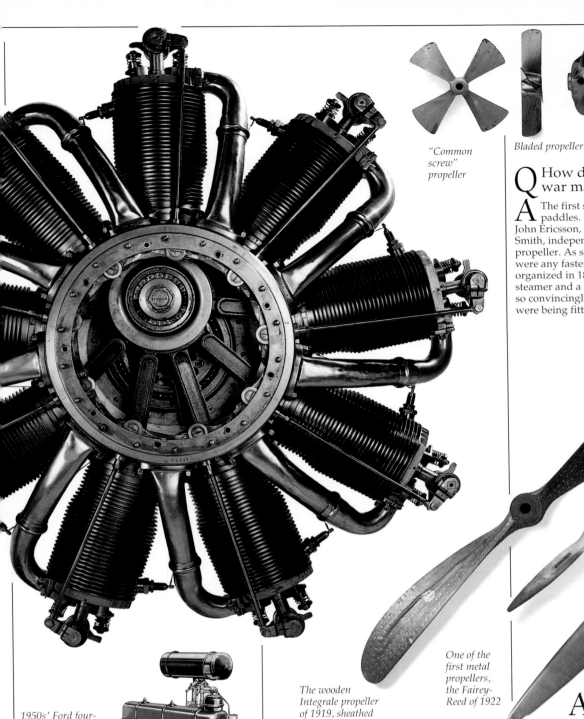

"Common screw" propeller

Bladed propeller

Mauretania's propellers

Q How did a tug-of-war make ships faster?

A The first steamships were driven by paddles. But in 1836, a Swedish engineer, John Ericsson, and British farmer, Francis Pettit Smith, independently invented the screw propeller. As so few people believed that screws were any faster than paddles, a tug-of-war was organized in 1845 between a screw-driven steamer and a paddle steamer. The screw won so convincingly that soon most new steamships were being fitted with screw propellers.

Variable pitch propeller to provide good thrust for take-off

1950s' Ford four-cylinder engine

The wooden Integrale propeller of 1919, sheathed in brass armour

One of the first metal propellers, the Fairey-Reed of 1922

Q Why are aircraft propellers twisted?

A Because they go round faster at the tips than they do near the centre. If the propeller blade was the same angle at the tip as it is at the centre, the air resistance on the tip would be too much, either slowing the propeller down or bending the blade. Making the blade twisted makes sure the air resistance is the same on the entire surface.

Q Who invented car engines?

A The petrol and diesel engines used in almost all electric vehicles are called internal combustion engines because they get their power from the combustion, or burning, of fuel inside the cylinders. They were invented by a Frenchman, Etienne Lenoir, in 1862.

Q Why do most jet airliners use turbofan jet engines?

A The simplest jets, turbojets, work by pushing a jet of hot air out behind them. In a turbofan engine, the hot-air jet is combined with the backdraught from a multi-bladed fan. Turbofans are much quieter and cheaper to run than turbojets. The immense fan provides much of the engine's power, especially at low speeds. In this Rolls-Royce Tay engine, the fan provides three times as much power as the hot-air jet.

59

Did cars or trains come first?

Why did early trains need a tall chimney?

The *Agenoria*, shown here, was built in 1829. Like most early steam locomotives, it looked very similar to the very first working steam locomotive built by Richard Trevithick in 1804, which had four wheels like a cart, a short tube-shaped boiler and a very tall smokestack, or chimney. A tall chimney improved the draught on the fire and made the locomotive more efficient – but there could be no low bridges on the line.

TRAINS AND CARS are much older than you might think. The basic principle of a railway dates back over 5,000 years ago to the ancient Sumerians, who cut grooves in stone roadways to guide wheeled vehicles along a straight course. Surprisingly, though, the first mechanically powered land transport was a car, not a train. The first car, a massive steam-driven carriage built by Frenchman Nicolas Cugnot, was built in 1769. The first railway locomotive was not built until 1804.

What did it mean if both signal arms were down?

In the days before coloured lights, train drivers were guided by semaphore signals. If both arms were down, they had to stop. If the upper arm only was raised, they could proceed cautiously. If both arms were raised the line ahead was all clear.

Mechanical semaphore signal

Folding hood

How did American settlers travel west in the 19th century?

Without cars or trains, the first settlers in America had to rely on wagons covered with canvas to travel the long distances to the American west. Each wagon was drawn by a pair of horses, and several wagons would travel together with scores of other settlers in a long wagon train. An escort was paid to offer protection and guidance.

Folding windscreen for rear seat passenger

Second-class compartment from a 1904 carriage

Why did early train passengers loosen their belts in stations?

For safety, the compartment doors on many trains have no handle on the inside. In early trains, the window was fastened by a simple leather belt and buckle. So passengers had to loosen the buckle and lean out of the window to open the door. This changed after World War II.

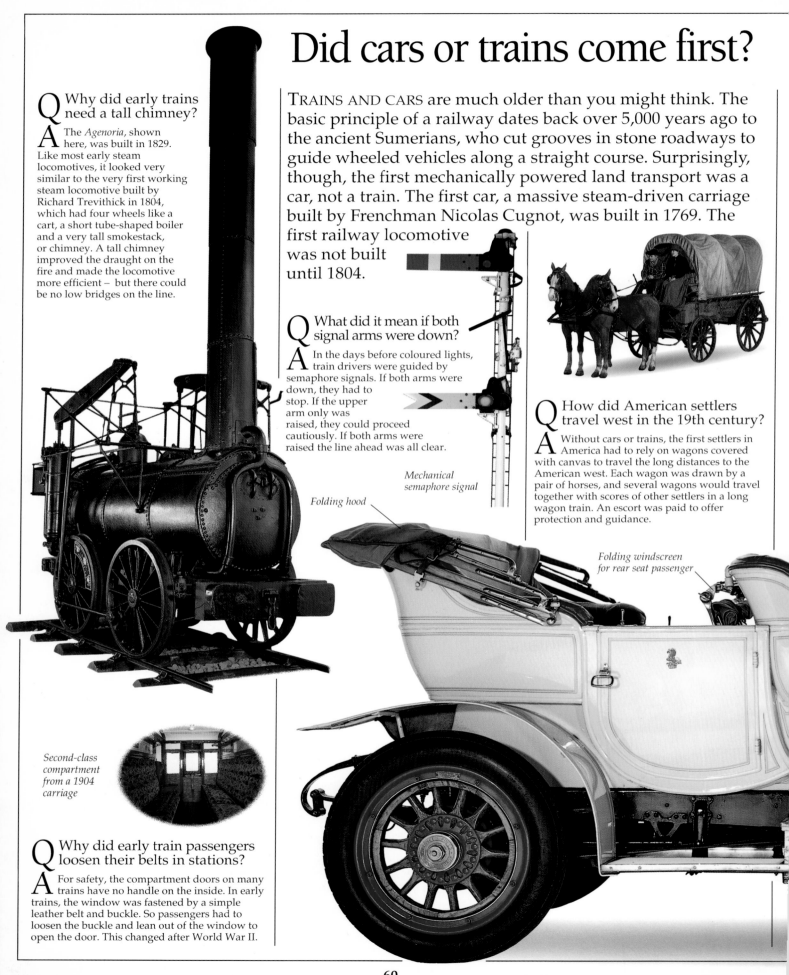

Early wheels were solid wooden discs | *Tripartite wheels were made of three pieces of wood* | *Stone wheels were used where wood was scarce* | *Dystrop wheels had sections cut out to make them lighter* | *Open wheels could be strengthened with cross-bars*

Q How long ago was the first wheel used?

A The wheel is one of the most important of all inventions. Wheels were probably first used 5,000 years ago in Mesopotamia, part of modern Iraq, both on carts to move big loads and by potters to help work clay.

Q Who invented the bicycle and when?

A The first bicycle was called a velocipede and was invented by a Scottish blacksmith in 1839. Despite its name, the velocipede was very slow: the back wheel turned at exactly the same rate as the pedals which were linked to the wheel not by a chain as on modern bikes but by connecting rods. The "safety bicycle" on which most modern bikes are based was introduced in the 1870s by James Starley of Coventry.

Pre-war racing cars looked like ordinary road cars

Q Why are racing cars faster than ordinary cars?

A Not only do racing cars have much more powerful engines than ordinary cars, but they are made of modern, ultralight materials and are so low slung that they almost scrape the ground. The body is also carefully streamlined to cut air resistance and shaped so that the air flowing over the car helps keep the car stable and on the road. Huge, wide tyres give extra grip at high speeds.

Roll bar to protect driver's head in a crash

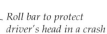

Wide, treadless tyres, called slicks, give extra grip on dry race circuits

Electric sidelight   *Rear oil lamp*

Q How did early motorists make sure they were seen at night?

A From 1899 on, many cars carried dim oil lamps for driving at night. But for many years they were considered luxury items. It was not until the 1930s that bright electric lights were standard equipment on most cars.

Q What was the first Rolls Royce called and when was it made?

A Charles Rolls and Henry Royce made one of their first cars in 1906, and the sheer quality of craftsmanship earned it the description of "the best car in the world". Its ghost-like quietness and shiny aluminium body suggested the name "Silver Ghost". The Silver Ghost shown here is a 40/50 from 1909.

"Spirit of Ecstasy" mascot

Handbrake

How do we fly?

IN CHINA thousands of years ago, people were carried up into the air by giant kites. But the first long, powered flight was made by the American brothers Orville and Wilbur Wright as recently as 1903. Since then nearly all flying machines have been based on the same principle. Specially shaped wings provide lift as they slice through the air, and an engine supplies the power to keep pushing the aeroplane through the air.

Q What are the smallest powered aircraft?

A Microlights, which were developed from hang-gliders in the 1970s. Many still have flexible delta-shaped fabric wings like hang-gliders with a simple tricycle dangling beneath. Others, especially in the USA and Australia, are more like aeroplanes and have fixed wings and wing flaps so they can climb or dive.

Q How did early pilots know where they were going?

A The only instrument most early pilots had was a compass, so they found their way simply by aiming for landmarks such as church steeples. In the Deperdussin cockpit here, the view ahead is obscured by the fuel tank, and the pilot had to lean out to check height and direction.

Q How did the first pilots know how high they were?

A The first aeroplanes had no instruments, so to find their height, or altitude, pilots would use little pocket altimeters such as the Elliot shown here. These were very similar to altimeters used by mountaineers for years before and worked simply by responding to changes in air pressure.

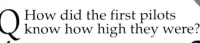

Q Why do jet airliners need stressmen?

A Because of the enormous pressure differences they must withstand at high altitudes, airliner bodies have to be tough as well as light – and even a tiny weakness could spell disaster. So the strength and durability of every minute section is carefully assessed – an enormous task once involving scores of stressmen but now made much easier by computers. There are hoop frames and stringers that run along the inside of the aircraft body, but these are small and much of the plane's strength comes from its metal skin.

Q What was the first craft to carry people over Paris?

A On 21 November 1783, Jean Pilâtre de Rozier and the Marquis d'Arlandes became Europe's first aeronauts when the Montgolfiers' balloon, filled with hot air, carried them into the skies above Paris. Within a fortnight a second flight was made, but this time the balloon was filled with hydrogen. Hot-air balloons disappeared for 170 years until they were revived in the 1960s. Hot-air ballooning is now a popular sport.

Duck flying

Q What is the black box?

A The black box is a special flight data recorder carried by all modern airliners and military aircraft. It is connected to all the aircraft's main systems and records everything that happens during a flight, monitoring instruments, radio messages, engine data and so on. If the plane crashes, the box is strong enough to survive, providing experts with a complete history of the flight so the cause of the accident can be found.

Q Why are sycamore seeds like helicopters?

A Helicopter rotor blades are like rotating wings. As they turn they generate enough lift to keep the helicopter in the air. Sycamore seeds are a similar shape and when they fall off the tree, they too whirl round and round to the ground.

Q How do wings enable birds to fly?

A Birds fly either by gliding with their wings held almost still or by flapping their wings up and down. Since gliding is much less tiring than flapping, birds that stay in the air for a long time, like birds of prey, tend to be good gliders. Even gliding birds flap their wings from time to time, though, if only for landing and take-off. For the downstroke, the bird's main wing feathers are closed together providing maximum push on the air. For the upstroke, the feathers open to allow the air to flow gently through.

Q What were dogfights?

A Dogfights were mid-air fights between single-seat scout planes in World War I. These planes usually had a single fixed forward-facing machine gun. This meant the pilot had to aim the whole aircraft at the enemy to shoot, so flying skill was vital. World War I "aces" such as Baron von Richthofen, the Red Baron, became famous for their exploits.

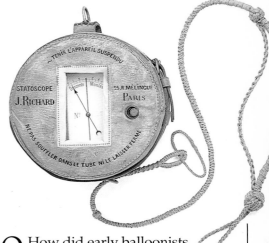

Q How did early balloonists keep a steady height?

A The first balloonists carried a pressure-sensitive instrument called a statoscope which told them immediately they began to rise or fall. If the balloon rose too much the balloonist had to let gas out, which wasted precious gas; if it sank too low, they had to throw out sand ballast. Constant rising and falling in this way soon cut short a flight.

The Blériot planes were the first successful monoplanes (single-winged planes)

Q Who made the first flight across the English Channel?

A Louis Blériot on 25 July 1909. Blériot made the 41-km (26-mile) flight in one of his own machines, a Blériot Type XI, identical to the one shown here. After the flight, Blériot became a celebrity overnight and, when more than 100 of the Type XI were ordered, he became the world's first major aircraft manufacturer.

63

Index

A

accordion 43
acorn 12
aircraft 58, 62-63
altimeter 62
amethyst 9
ammonites 25, 26
amphora 24, 29
amulet 50
anaethetic 51
anemone 15, 21
anthracite 26
Aphrodite 30
Apollo 31
Archer, Frederick Scott 54
architecture 29
armadillo 14
arrow 32, 46
asbestos 8
Asclepius 50
Australopithecine 27
axe 46

B

Babylon 29
Bacchus 9
badminton 41
Baird, John Logie 52
baldric 25
balloon 62, 63
banknotes 34, 35
bark (tree) 12, 13
barometer 7
baseball 41
battery 58
battle axe 49
beaver 20
beer 33
beetles 17, 19, 23, 25, 28
Bell, Alexander G. 53
Bentley, Wilson W. 7
Berliner, Emile 43
beryl 9
bicycle 61
birds 23, 63
black box 63
Blériot, Louis 63
boat 13, 56
bones 18-19
bow 46, 49
boxing 40
Boyle, Charles 7
bread 32
bridge 18, 19
brooch 38, 39
buckle 25
bullet 48
butterfly 16, 23

C

cactus 15
camel 35
camera 54
camouflage 16-17
canoe 13

car 19, 44, 59, 60-61
caravel 37
castanets 43
castor oil 51
caterpillar 23
chameleon 16
chisel 46
chiton 39
chloroplast 10
Christianity 31
chronometer 24, 37
chrysalis 16
cinchona 12
cinnabar 8
civilization 28
clothes 17, 18, 38-39, 47
coal 26
cobra 14
cockpit 45, 62
coins 24, 25, 34, 35
Colosseum 40
Colt, Samuel 48
Columbus, C. 37
communication 52-53
compass 25, 37, 62
conifer 12
Cook, James 25, 36, 37
corbita 35
Cortés, Hernán 37
corundum 9
crab 17, 20-21
crinoline 39
crops 32
cross-staff 36
crossbow 49
crystal 8, 9, 57

D

Daguerre, Louis 55
damselfly 11
Darius the Great 24, 29
De Forest, Lee 52
diamond 9
Diana (goddess) 9
Diaz, Bartolomeu 37
Dickson, William 54
dinosaur 26-27, 43
dolphin 39
drill 45, 47, 50
drug 12, 50, 51
drum 24, 42, 52
duck 4, 18
dye 39, 47

E

Earth 6
Eastman, George 54
Edison Thomas 43, 53, 54
egg 22-23
Egyptians 12, 25, 28, 30-31, 33, 35, 50
electricity 58
elephant 5, 18-19, 57,
emerald 9
emu 23
engine 44, 45, 58-59
Ericsson, John 59
Erikson, Leif 36
eye-shadow 28
eyes, fish 17
eyespot 16

F

false teeth 45, 50
fencing 41
fern 26
Fertile Crescent 32
film 54
fire 27, 47, 55
fish 15, 16, 17, 33, 36
flea 57
Fleming, John Ambrose 52
flowers 4, 10, 11, 26
food 32, 33
foxglove 51
Franklin, Sir John 47
frog 5, 14, 16, 19, 58
fruit 11, 32
fungus 10, 11

G

Galilei, Galileo 6
Galvani, Luigi 58
games 28, 40-41
gearwheel 47
germ 51
gladiator 40
goddesses 9, 30-31
gods 9, 28, 30-31, 50
gold 8, 31, 34, 35, 39
gramophone 43
granite 8
grape 33
Greeks 24, 29, 30-31, 40
gremlin 55
guillemot 22
gunpowder 48
Gutenberg J. 52

H

Hapi 28
harp 42-43
Harrison, John 37
hedgehog 15
helicopter 63
helmet 49
Henry VIII 39
Henson, William 58
Hippocrates 50
Hittites 34
Homo habilis 46
hornet 15
horse 56
Horus 31
humans 19, 27

I J K L

Iguandon 26
Inuit (Eskimos) 47
iron 34
jade 9
jellyfish 15
jewellery 31, 39
key 29
Khepri 28
Khnum 28
Kingsley, Mary 36
kit (violin) 42
kiwi 23
knife 47
Kodak 54

lapis lazuli 35
laurel 10
Le Prince, Louis 54
leaves 5, 13
Leeuwenhoek, A. van 51
Lenoir, Etienne 59
lights, car 61
lionfish 4, 14
liverwort 10
Livingstone, David 36, 37
lock 29
longship 36
Louis XIV 9
"Lucy" 27
lute 42

M

magnolia 11, 26
mammoth 27
Marathon 40
marble 9
Marconi, Gugliemo 52
Medusa 30, 31
menorah 31
mermaid's purse 22
microlight 62
microscope 51
moccasin 39
monotreme 22
Montgolfier brothers 62
morse code 45, 53
Morse, Samuel 53
Morton, William 51
mosquito 12
moss 10
moth 53
mountain 6
movies 54-55
mummy case 30
muscle 57
music 42-43

N O P

Nautilus 5
nest 20
oak 12
Olympic Games 40
opal 9
orrery 5, 7
panpipes 24, 42
papyrus 12, 28
Parasaurolophus 43
Pasteur, Louis 51
Pegasus 31
pen 12, 53
pepper 11
Persepolis 29
Perseus 30, 31
pheasant 23
Pheidippides 40
Phenakistoscope 55
pheromone 53
phonograph 43
photography 54-55
photosynthesis 10, 11
pigment 8
Pilâtre de Rozier, J. 62
pine cone 6
pistol 48-49
pitcher plant 10
Pizarro, Francisco 37

plaice 17
planet 6
plants 10-11
Plateau, Joseph 55
plough 32-33
plum 12
poison 14
polar bear 16
pollination 10, 11
Polo, Marco 36
pomegranate 32
post mill 56
printing 52
propeller 59
pufferfish 15
pump 58
puppet 55

Q R

quadrant 7, 36
quartz 8, 9, 57
quinine 12
racing car 61
radio 45, 52
recorder 42
revolver 44, 48
rhinoceros's horn 51
Richtofen, Baron von 63
rocks 8-9
Rolls, Charles 61
Romans 29, 31, 33, 35, 43, 51, 53
rowan berry 13
Royce, Henry 61
ruby 9

S

sail 56
salamander 4, 14-15
salmon 33
sandal 24, 28
Savery, Thomas 58
scabbard 28-29
scalpel 9
scarab 25, 28
Scissa 33
Scott, Robert 36
scurvy 36
sea urchin 26
seeds 11, 12, 13, 63
Seguin brothers 58
semaphore 53, 60
sequoia 12
sextant 37
shark 26
shepherd 25, 33
ship 35, 36-37
shoe 39, 41
Silver Ghost 60-61
skeleton 18-19, 27
skull 19
Smith, Francis Pettit 59
snail 21
snake 5, 14, 16, 22
snowflake 7
softball 41
spark plug 58
spider 15
spiny anteater 22
squirrel 20
Starley, James 61

steam 58-59
stick insect 4, 16
stirrup jar 35
Stone Age 27, 46
Stringfellow, John 58
stylus 53
sugar 56
Sun 7, 56
sundial 7
surgery 51
sword 41, 48

T

tarantula 15
Taynton, Bill 52
telephone 44, 53
television 52
tennis racket 41
termite 41
terrapin 21
thermometer 6
thunderstone 26
tiger 17
tiger's eye 8
toad 22-23
tortoise 21
track shoe 41
train 60
trees 12-13
Trevithick, Richard 60
Triceratops 27
trumpet 42
tsaung 42-43
turbojet 59
turtle 18, 21

V

Vandals 39
velocipede 61
Venus' flytrap 11
Venus (goddess) 30
Vikings 36, 49
violin 42
volcanic eruption 7, 57
Volta, Alessandro 58
votive offering 50

W Z

wagon 35,60
wasp 20
water melon 33
Watt, James 44, 58
weapon 27, 48-49
weather 6
weather cock 7
wedjat eye 28
weightlifter 57
weights & measures 35
Wells, Horace 51
whalebone 18
wheel 45, 61
whelk shell 20-21
wine 33
wings 62, 63
wrasse 16
Wright Brothers 62
writing 53
Zeus 31
zodiac 29

Acknowledgements

Dorling Kindersley would like to thank:
Helena Spiteri for editorial assistance; Jean Cooke for the index; and the following museums for photography: British Museum; Museum of London; Museum of the Moving Image; Museum of Mankind; National Maritime Museum; Natural History Museum; National Motor Museum, Beaulieu; Pitt Rivers Museum; Royal Geographical Society; Science Museum; University Museum; University Museum of Architecture and Anthropology; Worthing Museum and Art Gallery.

Picture credits
t = top, b = bottom, c = centre, l = left, r = right

Ancient Art and Architecture Collection 31cl. Aviation Picture Library 62cl. Jane Burton 17cr. ET Archive 52tc. Michael Holford 30cl, 31br. Scala 31bc. Science Photo Library 7tl, tcl, tc. Bob Symes 57bl. Syndication International 56t.

Every effort has been made to trace the copyright holder and we apologise for any unintentional omissions. We would be pleased to insert the appropriate acknowledgement in any subsequent edition of this publication.